THE SAS
MENTAL ENDURANCE
HANDBOOK

Also Available from The Lyons Press:

The SAS Combat Handbook
The SAS Fighting Techniques Handbook
The SAS Guide to Tracking
The SAS Self-Defense Handbook
The SAS Tracking and Navigation Handbook

THE **SAS**
MENTAL ENDURANCE
HANDBOOK

CHRIS McNAB

THE LYONS PRESS

GUILFORD, CONNECTICUT

AN IMPRINT OF THE GLOBE PEQUOT PRESS

First Lyons Press edition, 2002

Copyright © 2001 by Amber Books Ltd

The Lyons Press is an imprint of The Globe Pequot Press.

Printed in Portugal

2   4   6   8   10   9   7   5   3

The Library of Congress Cataloging-in-Publication Data is available on file.

ISBN 1-58574-442-5

Contents

CHAPTER ONE

The Will to Survive

In the martial arts, the mental state should remain the same as normal. In ordinary circumstances as well as when practising martial arts, let there be no change in the state of mind – with the mind open and direct, neither tense nor unfocused, centring the thoughts so that there is no imbalance, calmly relax your mind, and savour this moment of peace.

Miyamoto Musashi,
The Book of Five Rings *(1643)*

Despite this opening quotation's mystical ring, it is actually about the brutal art of killing. It was written in the 17th century by the samurai warrior Miyamoto Musashi. Musashi was no detached philosopher – he killed his first man at the age of 13 – and he was intimately acquainted with the mental ability required to take the life of another individual and to guard your own in a violent duel. His vision was a strange mix of peace and aggression. In combat, he said, the mind should be quiet rather than angry, responding to attacks naturally without predicting results, the state of calm allowing the samurai to see everything clearly and not become clouded by furious emotion.

Musashi's recommendations for developing mental endurance in combat – the theme of this book – were practised by few in history and mastered by even fewer. Yet what Musashi was exploring was the fact that, in the critical seconds of combat, the mental state of the fighter can have a more decisive effect on the outcome of the fight than the weapons he wields. This was a conclusion to which the great military leader Sun Tzu also came, some 1500 years before Musashi, in relation to the performance of officers:

If officers are not thoroughly drilled, they will be anxious and confused in battle; if generals are not competently trained, they will suffer mental anguish when they face the enemy.
Sun Tzu, The Art of War

Here, Sun Tzu comes at the issue of mental performance from a different angle to Musashi, that of training. Training, Sun Tzu implies, should accustom the soldier's mind to face combat with resolution and not buckle under the impact of violence and chaos. Only when the mind is disciplined can the body follow it into battle.

Both Sun Tzu and Musashi were writing during the days when steel held in the hand still decided the outcome of many battles. Yet, even though there is an immeasurable contrast between those battles of the ancient past and the ultra hi-tech conflicts of the present, the fact remains that the role of the combat soldier is one of the most psychologically demanding professions. Whatever the period of history, the soldier in action must not only cope psychologically with the traumatic visions of death and mutilation surrounding him, but he must also come to terms with the fact that he himself may die or have to kill. On top of this, he must retain focus on his mission, staying sharp and responsive in the midst of incredible chaos, noise and aggression.

For those who master this level of mental control in war, the rewards can be extraordinary. It has long been noted by military strategists that a small group of highly motivated, focused and resilient men can overwhelm or resist a much larger group lacking such qualities. During Germany's early Blitzkrieg actions against the Low Countries in World War II, for example, it took only 85 highly trained and ruthless Fallschirmjäger paratroopers to capture the Belgian fortress Eben Emael, despite the fact that Eben Emael had a garrison of up to 2000 men, some 4.5km (2.7miles) of underground passages and a vast array of heavy gun, anti-aircraft and machine-gun emplacements. Similarly, when entire Iraqi companies encountered tiny SAS units during the Gulf War, so effective was the SAS response that panicked Iraqi soldiers reported that battalion-strength forces had attacked them.

The examples of mental force over physical strength are legion, yet our actual understanding of the relationship between mental capacity and combat ability is fairly recent, beginning in earnest during World War I. This book focuses on bringing out the lessons of nearly 100 years of research. Through concentrating on the fundamental aspects of military mental performance – resistance to combat stress, tactical intelligence, leadership and so on – we will look at the techniques derived to achieve the optimum state of mind for military efficiency. Some are fairly obvious; for instance, regular sleep must be observed to prevent deterioration in decision-making abilities and morale. Yet the research has also uncovered the unusual; for example, viewing an attacking aircraft through a hand formed like a telescope allows the viewer to make a more accurate judgement of its range. What is common to all the techniques included here is that they were born from the hard experience of the battlefield and thus are known to work in the most abject of circumstances.

THE CODES OF WAR

Prior to the 20th century, there was little explicit focus on mental development in the world's armed forces. The exception to this could well be the samurai tradition already noted. As well as practising Buddhist techniques of 'self-emptying' – living under the expectation of death and suffering until both of these influences held no fear – the samurai followed the code of bushido. One of the clearest descriptions of bushido came from Nitobe Inazo in 1905, who distilled centuries of samurai tradition into six virtues to which the samurai should aspire. These were duty (*giri*), humanity (*ninyo*), strength of spirit (*fudo*), magnanimity (*doryo*), resolution (*shiki*) and generosity (*ansha*). By ascribing to this set of values, the samurai, it was supposed, would not only attain moral virtue, but his mind would also attain the strength and power necessary for the warrior.

The code of bushido developed over centuries as a set of values which distinguished the warrior from those were not members of the elite. In varying ways, it is a form of 'mental training' through example that has accompanied elite soldiers from the most ancient of times until around the late-19th century. Casting our view back into the realms of Greek and Roman mythology, the Homeric and Virgilian heroes of Ajax, Achilles, Odysseus and Aeneas were archetypal warriors who acted in ancient society as models for what the warrior should be. This was, in effect, mental training through aspiring to be like these great figures. Uniting such elites as Xerxes' 'Immortals' of the fifth century BC, the Roman Praetorian guard, the Islamic warriors of the seventh century AD and Viking and Norman raiders is the principle that mental preparedness for combat is something learnt by emulating the warriors of old and striving to live up to the virtues of courage, determination and ruthless strength.

This trend is particularly visible in the standards of 'chivalry' which governed the field conduct of knights during the medieval period. Chivalry originated as a code around 1100 and acted like a form of bushido that was less death-centred. Values such as courage, loyalty, prudence and honour were

Samurai warrior

The Samurai saw combat as a natural extension of a strong and calm spirit, and they trained themselves to accept, and thus overcome, any fear of death.

Trooper 22 SAS

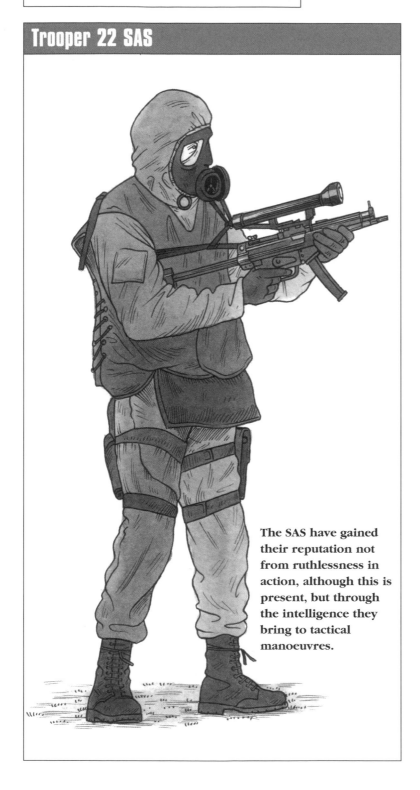

The SAS have gained their reputation not from ruthlessness in action, although this is present, but through the intelligence they bring to tactical manoeuvres.

mixed with stealth and intelligence in attack, and formed a set of expected behaviour which acted like a form of psychological training. How effective it was is difficult to tell, as much of the evidence comes from embellished myths and legends, rather than battlefield accounts. In a sense, however, this type of 'mental training' persisted until the end of World War I and perhaps even lingered into the next war.

The absurd image of the British Army officer leading his men at walking pace into the lethal spray of German heavy machine-guns carrying only a riding crop is a legacy of the supposed warrior virtues of the noble classes. Yet the hideous damage that the new weapons inflicted on the belief that spirit could triumph over technology was irreparable. The Western Front produced a massive increase in psychiatric casualties, with shell shock and personality disorders. This awoke Western medical authorities to the fact that the mind of a soldier could be damaged just like a physical organ.

MILITARY PSYCHOLOGY

The seeds of military psychology were sown when the nature of warfare itself changed in the early part of the 20th century. The sheer force of new military tactics and weapons, with huge

Typical equipment of the Spetsnaz soldier

Handling such a range of equipment requires excellent skills in organisation, technical knowledge and combat awareness, as well as a strong back.

Anti-tank Missile

Rucksack

Radio

Sniper Rifle

Grenades

Claymore Mine

Anti-personnel Mine

Rations

Water Bottle

Radar Detector

A range of SAS equipment

During the Gulf War, the SAS often carried 40kg (88lb) operational packs, which can lead to a lack of focus and concentration if the soldier is not fit enough to cope.

Bergen Rucksack

Anti-aircraft Missile

Silenced Sub-machine Gun

Claymore Mine

Radio

Maps and Compass

First Aid Kit

Knife

Survival Kit

Torch

Wire

Escape Belt

the qualities of the elite leader to focusing on the experience of the common soldier. As total war seemed to produce a disproportionate level of psychiatric casualties amongst these men, medical answers had to be found to prevent and cure the drain on manpower through combat fatigue and traumatic reactions. All of a sudden, the psychological collapse of a soldier during combat became an issue of mental health, rather than being about his lack of 'moral fibre' or 'manliness'.

One of the earliest nations to catch on to this message was Russia. During the Russo-Japanese War of 1904–05, Russian psychologists and mental health experts actually went to the front with the combatants to offer treatment. By World War I, psychologists were increasingly becoming part of regular army units, giving treatments to mentally injured soldiers which ranged from the considerate to the barbaric (soldiers struck dumb by trauma, for instance, were often given electric shocks of increasing severity until they spoke again).

destruction and mobility becoming the dominant conditions, meant that massed armies were required on a scale never before seen. This brought about a shift of emphasis from

Between 1915 and 1916, the Allied Medical Services recognised that most incidences of shell shock were actually cases of psychological collapse, and should be treated as such. When the United States entered the war in 1917, the American Psychological Association was already considering ways of applying psychological testing and treatment to shape battlefield performance. Mental tests such as the US Army's Alpha and Beta tests were instigated to screen recruits for mental characteristics and place them in the appropriate military jobs. Testing then proliferated into other areas of military life. Leadership, intelligence, tactical skills, emotional resilience – all aspects of the military personality came under the psychologist's gaze. It should be noted that there was no equivalent acceptance of psychological disorder from the German military. The idea that the German soldier should become mentally incapacitated was anathema to the German warrior culture and so psychological casualties were generally treated either as cowards or as physically damaged in some way. This outlook persisted throughout World War II; some 15,000 German soldiers were court-martialled and executed for what we now know as psychiatric disorders.

GROWING SUCCESS

As treatments advanced – by the end of the war, 60 per cent of Allied psychiatric casualties were successfully returned to the front – so did the understanding of how to design training and military organisation to prevent mental problems and produce more efficient fighters. The interwar period was marked by a reduction in investigation into military psychology in general, although the postwar problems of many soldiers returning to civilian life did provide a new vision of the longer term effects of combat trauma. Yet the defining moment of the development of military psychology was just around the corner.

World War II produced an explosion of psychological research on an unparalleled scale; indeed, military psychology became the largest sector of mental health studies in the United States. War was growing ever more complex in its weaponry, tactics and communications, and the mental demands this produced led to a major investment in improving the performance of the individual combat soldier. After some of the early battles in North Africa, the Allies were shocked at just what effects modern warfare could have on the common soldier. Aid stations started to receive men who had to be led around by the hand like children, or who would defecate uncontrollably at any sudden, loud noise. Others were rendered completely catatonic or would lose the ability to speak or to move one of their limbs.

New programmes of treatment were designed to cope with these terrible mental injuries. On the whole, these programmes saw a high percentage of casualties restored to health, but they were much needed. Of all Allied medical evacuations, 23 per cent were psychiatric (compared with only six per cent in the subsequent Korean War). Although in part owing to the hugely traumatic nature of total war, this was also because the massive level of conscription allowed a greater number of personality disorders to slip past screening into the military ranks. Greater questions were being raised over the whole screening process in recruitment and a truism was discovered that holds good to this day – it is impossible to predict from screening who will submit to combat trauma and who will not (although present-day analysis does give a higher degree of certainty).

The treatment of psychiatric casualties was naturally an urgent priority; however, now military psychology was not exclusively about preventing mental problems, but also focused on making the human machine perform at its best in a multitude of roles. Thus, the range of topics studied greatly expanded to include morale, environmental effects on fighting ability, the psychological effects of different weapons, the use of propaganda, selecting personnel for special missions and personality types. World War II gave the 20th century much of its understanding about how the human mind works in combat. It also introduced many common terms for psychological conditions related to soldiering. Perhaps the most significant of these was 'exhaustion', a term which referred to psychological and physical disintegration beyond the limits of individual's endurance. The great distances and varied terrain covered in World War II made this an acute problem; the attempt to solve it led to a better appreciation of how an unstable mind and an exhausted body feed off one another. Also, apart from the obvious strains of physical effort and combat shock, psychologists and psychiatrists noted many non-combat-related phenomena which contributed to mental disturbance in soldiers. These included factors such as the quality of leadership, the access to comrade support, separation from family and home, and also the problems that could arise from nervousness about future combat.

INTEGRAL MENTAL TRAINING AND TREATMENT

When World War II ended, psychological assessment, training and treatment were a fully-fledged and integral part of military life. Not only was there a much better comprehension of what was required to keep men sane and stable in the 'fog of war', but there was also a new understanding of how to foster the soldier's mind as part of his essential weaponry. Both these lessons went on to inform training in conflicts such as Korea and Vietnam, and with each new conflict fresh insights were gained into the art of war and soldiering. Work during World War II had laid the foundations for much of our understanding about phenomena such as combat stress, exhaustion (or 'combat fatigue', as it became known), leadership qualities and interpersonal influences on mental state; however, post–World War II military conflicts have presented demands of a type rarely encountered prior to 1945.

Vietnam was, perhaps, the watershed between the old and new style of wars. US combat soldiers in Vietnam faced many unusual and troubling pressures. First, they experienced a form of conflict in which an ambush would wrench them from extreme boredom to extreme violence in seconds, only to subside quickly and leave nothing but the horrors of the injured and the dead behind. Occasionally, full-scale Vietcong or NVA attacks would interrupt this pattern. In places such as the Central Highlands and areas around the DMZ, these attacks made battlefield landscapes akin to those of France and Belgium during World War I. As the war lost its popular support worldwide, the soldiers in the field came to feel that they did not have the backing of the people at home. Drugs and alcohol were freely available and the logistical might of the United States made the soldiers live in a curious no-man's land between third-world poverty and the painful nostalgia of the comforts of home. Weaponry became ever more brutal and the Vietnamese heat kept soldiers teetering on the brink of sunstroke and dehydration.

The much-publicised atrocities committed by US soldiers in Vietnam awoke many to the fact that wars and soldiering had changed utterly. Although actual numbers of psychiatric casualties in Vietnam were relatively small – about five per cent of the medical evacuations – the cohesion amongst units often seemed lost and this was taking a dramatic psychological toll on performance. 'Fragging' – the killing of one's officers using fragmentation grenades – reached almost epidemic proportions in some units. Also, standard military training did not prepare soldiers for the great cultural transformation of operating in Southeast Asia. By the end of the conflict, military psychologists realised that they would have to broaden the focus of their work. Cultural attitudes, feelings about race and gender, the relationship between

British Army Intelligence Test, 1940s

In the example given to the right, the total of each row is 12. This is the same whether the row is formed horizontally, vertically or diagonally.

Complete the boxes laid out below, following the same principles, but to the totals given underneath each of the boxes.

3	2	7
8	4	0
1	6	5

Total: 15

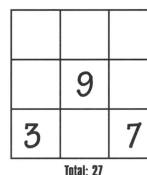

Total: 27

Total: 39

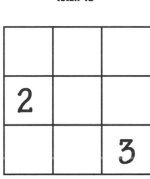

Use 2,3,4,5,6,7,8,9,10 Total: 18

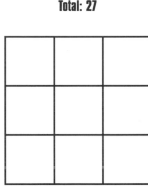

Use 4,5,6,7,8,9,10 Total: 24

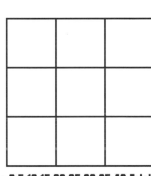

Use 0,5,10,15,20,25,30,35,40 Total: 60

drugs and fighting ability, morale and political cause, the strain of handling advanced technology – many new factors fed into the understanding of how soldiers perform and how treatment and training techniques had to keep pace. Vietnam focused attention on the soldier in his broadest possible context, from his beliefs to his bravery, examining how the qualities he possesses fit into the operational situation.

The lessons of Vietnam were taken forwards into subsequent conflicts. Following wars such as those fought in the Falklands and the Gulf, in recent years the focus has shifted towards realistic training methods which partially 'battleproof' the soldier and make him less shocked by the actuality of combat. Most military mental training is now designed to produce soldiers who are intelligent and thoughtful individuals, with adaptability taking equal importance with courage and strength of mind. The modern soldier must have the mental capacity to switch from aggressive fighting patrols to food distribution in a matter of hours, even minutes, a phenomenon that the US Marines label the 'three-block war' – you can literally go from combat to non-combat duties in the space of three blocks. Today, peacekeeping and humanitarian actions are presenting the

Choosing semi/full-automatic fire

Psychologists found that at under 25m (82ft) soldiers achieved better kill ratios with automatic fire, and over 50m (164ft) with semi-automatic.

psychological challenge of how to keep soldiers motivated in combat areas where they are not actually allowed to participate in the fighting, even if grave crimes against civilians are being committed within visual range. In light of the recent experiences in Yugoslavia and Somalia, this will no doubt be a theme of investigation for many years to come.

THE ELITE FIGHTING MIND

Somewhere along the line, all soldiers from most nations have benefited from the knowledge of military psychology. Yet where do the elite soldiers, those at the very top of military practice, fit into this equation? In one sense, it is difficult to know, as elite units such as the US Navy SEALs, the British SAS, the Israeli Sayeret Mat'kal and the Italian Combusin are among the most secretive organisations in the world. Most elite unit research into psychological techniques is highly classified, even work that was done back in the 1940s and 1950s. Yet details have started to filter down through autobiographies, independent research and, most importantly, those units which have an elite capability, but which do not have the same protective cloak of secrecy. Examples would include the US Marines, the US Rangers, the Royal Marines, the Israeli and British paratroopers, the Italian Alpini and many other infantry and specialist fighting squads around the world. Such units tend to have a strong intellectual interchange with other special forces and actively borrow techniques. Thus these techniques become more visible to the outside world.

In order to understand the nature of elite unit psychological training, it is worth reminding ourselves why such units were born in the first place. Special forces – units created to perform advanced duties beyond the capability of the average soldier – have been with us since the beginning of military history in one form or another. Yet, prior to the 20th century, elite units tended to take their place alongside the ranks of other units in conventional battles. Special forces as we know them today are another matter. In the immediate aftermath of World War II, many of the elite units that had been developed for covert operations were disbanded, including the SAS. However, the Cold War, and upheaval in the colonies of European nations quickly followed the war's end. Short of outright war in many instances, military establishments around the globe soon recognised the need for small groups of soldiers with supreme fighting ability to fight the new wars of counterterrorism, counterinsurgency, small-scale wars and espionage. Many units would be created in response to a specific international challenge, only achieving permanence once they had proved their ruthless worth.

Especially pertinent to our discussion of military psychology is the emergence of US Army Special Forces in the early 1950s. In 1952, the Psychological Warfare Centre was established, its base at Fort Bragg, North Carolina. The remit of psychological warfare extended into the realms of counterinsurgency and spying, and thus the centre gathered units of uniquely trained men to perform such missions. The growth in such units provided the context for the emergence of official special forces squads and, on 20 June 1952, the 10th Special Forces Group (SFG) was established at Fort Bragg, the 77th SFG emerging just over a year later.

The link between psychological warfare and special forces suggests the distinct requirements of elite forces for men and women who exhibit exceptional intelligence, as well as almost superhuman endurance in the execution of their missions. The US Army Special Forces would go on to prove these qualities in Vietnam during their main operational programme, the setting up of Civilian Irregular Defense Groups (CIDG) in co-operation with South Vietnamese civilians, the ARVN and the Montagnard mountain dwellers. This programme not only required counterinsurgency skills in a jungle environment, but also necessitated formidable social skills in building understanding and trust with the Vietnamese. The enormous flexibility demanded of the Green Berets, the frequent political sensitivity of their missions and the self-reliance required to complete such missions meant that only the best could pass through training to become full-fledged Special Forces warriors.

The US Army Special Forces soldier is typical of the requirements for elite soldiers worldwide. An SAS soldier, for example, can be expected to possess one or two extra

Psychology of knife design

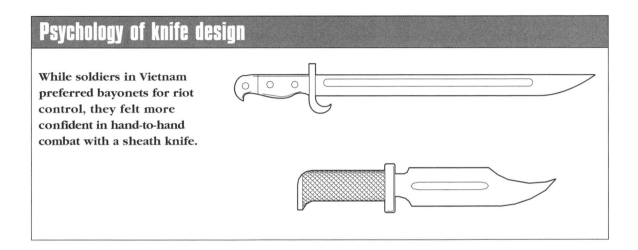

While soldiers in Vietnam preferred bayonets for riot control, they felt more confident in hand-to-hand combat with a sheath knife.

Judging distance

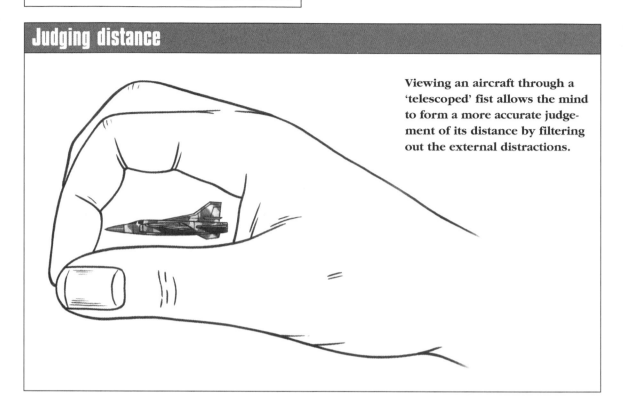

Viewing an aircraft through a 'telescoped' fist allows the mind to form a more accurate judgement of its distance by filtering out the external distractions.

languages and specialist understanding of military applications such as communications, demolitions, combat medicine, parachuting, diving or marksmanship. Naturally, recruiters for such units look for individuals with minds that can handle such a multitude of skills in a life-or-death setting.

The actual psychological testing procedures of elite units are highly confidential. What we do know is that there is a defined body of psychological qualities that are common to most elite squads. This is not to say that there is conformity amongst elite personnel – indeed, special forces soldiers are usually selected on the basis of their individuality – but all elite soldiers will be found to possess the following attributes.

Intelligence
All soldiers must display intelligence, but, in elite units, it must be to a heightened

degree. Even in large-scale elite units such as the US Marines, with 172,000 personnel on active duty, about 90 per cent of their entrants are high school graduates. This predisposes the Marine Corps towards excellent decision-making skills at every level of rank and operation. Also, studies conducted in the 1950s discovered that men who committed themselves to battle with greater motivation had a mean IQ of 91, whereas those that hung back from the fight or displayed indecision had a mean IQ of 78. Ironically, in most regular military units, those with lower IQs are usually sent into combat; however, a capable intelligence is a must for elite units.

Self-Control
Self-control is perhaps the primary virtue of a special forces soldier. Whereas regular military forces often operate in large-scale units

or movements, elite units tend to work in small squads or even as individuals. This means that each soldier must be able to execute a demanding mission with little or no external pressure to perform. Instead, his or her self-discipline will be the impetus behind the mission's success. Elite forces can also spend a great deal of time in static observation and reconnaissance missions, so must be able to deal with the crushing boredom of long, solitary watches, while maintaining an alert attitude.

Ruthlessness

Special forces soldiers sometimes have to perform some of the most unpalatable operations of all military forces, operations which require great violence to be imposed upon the enemy without mercy or relief. During the Moluccan train incident – a Dutch train was hijacked in 1977 by terrorists demanding independence for the Molucca Islands – hand-picked Royal Dutch Marines stormed the train and slaughtered six of the nine terrorists. The killing took place in a matter of only seconds, the marines using their automatic weapons against the enemy with brutal efficiency. Two hostages were also killed in the interchange of fire. The successful action illustrates

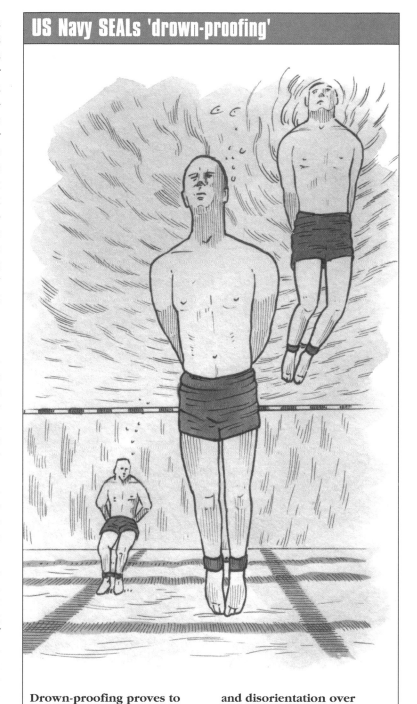

US Navy SEALs 'drown-proofing'

Drown-proofing proves to the instructors that the SEAL recruit can manage stress and disorientation over long periods without panic or confusion.

that combat must be prosecuted with an absolute disdain for the lives of the enemy, yet each soldier must keep his aggression controlled to avoid lethal errors.

Knowledge

One of the defined duties for a US Marine is to become 'a lifelong student of the Art of War'. This stipulation is typical of elite forces worldwide, in which a high precedent is placed on their soldiers being acutely well informed about military history, tactics, international politics and foreign cultures, as well as having a heightened knowledge of combat craft. A typical test for this general awareness can be found in officer recruitment for units such as the Royal Marines. In this test, a member of the examining board points to an unlabelled country on a map of the world and the recruit must identify the country and talk for one or two minutes on the cultural and political situation within that country. Knowledge of foreign cultures and languages is also especially valuable, as this allows a soldier to function more easily on foreign operations and develop a more intelligent basis to his or her actions.

Resistance to Physical Discomfort

Because many special forces operations are conducted well away from the logistical support of main forces, powers of endurance must be formidable. Not only must special forces soldiers be able to withstand traversing long distances on foot and at speed, but they also must be prepared for the capture and violent interrogation which threaten all elite operatives. The skill of mentally dismissing physical pain is usually created and tested during exhausting training. An example of this is the US Navy SEALs' 'Hell Week', a period of seven days which recruits spend almost entirely without sleep and usually immersed in freezing water. One peculiar aspect of this training is 'drown proofing'. This is where the soldier is dropped into a swimming pool with wrists and ankles bound, after which the recruit must keep afloat for 20 minutes and then perform underwater exercises (still with arms and legs tied) for another 10 minutes before swimming 100m (100 yards). Such training is not simply a form of torture (although many SEALs would disagree), but also actually allows the trainers to see if the soldier has the mental fortitude to keep pushing through what seems like interminable discomfort. Only when this is proved can unit members have the confidence that their personnel will never give in to adversity and will push themselves to the limit to achieve mission objectives.

These are just some of the mental qualities demanded of the special forces soldier; it is these and others which are the focus of this book. Psychological training aims to instil an exceptional degree of motivation and produce soldiers who are less susceptible to adverse combat reactions and more inclined to pursue their military goals despite any surrounding danger, no matter how hazardous. It also serves to debunk conventional wisdom. A good non-military example would be that some US police departments found that their officers were adopting TV tactics in a gunfight, frequently ending up killed or wounded as a result. Training had to be amended so that the officers were aware of this subconscious tactical predisposition and were also capable of overriding it with proper manoeuvres.

The same applies to military training, especially in the elite units. Special forces are trained to look beyond the conventional and that is why they are so feared – their patterns of behaviour are difficult for the enemy to predict. By understanding how their own minds work, they know how their enemies' minds work. Thus it is that psychological training is not simply a tool for mental resilience; it is, in essence, part of the elite soldier's arsenal.

Fighter or non-fighter

During World War II and the 1950s, several studies were commissioned to judge what distinguished fighters from non-fighters. S. L. A. Marshall produced a hotly contested study in the late 1940s which singled out fighters as men who actively threw themselves into the battle, engaging the enemy with their weapons from the start. This was opposed to non-fighters, who tended to take a passive role in action, often not firing their weapons at all. This was drawn from Marshall's conclusion that, in World War II, only around 15 per cent of an Allied company would actually fire their weapons in combat. Marshall's conclusions were expanded by further research from the Personnel Research Branch of the US Army's Adjutant General and the Human Resources Research Office. Their research was carried out in the context of the Korean War and consisted of an exhaustive series of interviews and testing procedures on actual combat units. From these studies, and from subsequent research which was carried out both in the United States and abroad, the following distinctions emerged:

FIGHTER

● Tends to engage in violent actions without requiring external pressure
● Instinctively pursues leadership roles either as a function of his rank or in the absence of the usual squad leader
● Maintains composure and clear thought processes even under fire
● Accepts responsibility for his actions
● Tends to be supportive of the group as a whole
● Usually possesses a higher rank than non-fighters
● Generally of higher intelligence than non-fighters. Mean IQ of 91
● A higher percentage of fighters are regular army, rather than draftees
● Displays an independent personality resistant to depression. Capable of being spontaneous and avoids introversion
● Has a strong sense of humour
● Family background tends to be financially and emotionally stable. Parents often engaged in running their own businesses
● Faster reaction times than the non-fighter
● Generally taller and heavier than non-fighters
● Tends to do well at physical sports

NON-FIGHTER

● Plays a minimal part in any combat, tending to withdraw away from action when it takes place
● Becomes psychologically reticent under fire and needs strong external motivation (for example, orders, immediate threat to life, etc.) to perform
● Overimaginative, seeing matters as he imagines them, rather than seeing them as they really are
● Avoids performing duties, idle
● Succumbs to mental terrors and is prone to psychological problems
● Generally less intelligent than fighters. Mean IQ of 78
● In some research, 40 per cent of non-fighters had lost their fathers before they reached the age of 18
● More financially constrained background. Often had to contribute to the family income from an earlier age
● Tends to be interested in the opposite sex from an earlier age than fighters
● Has more financial obligations to family than the fighter while in service
● More prone to periods of depression and despondency

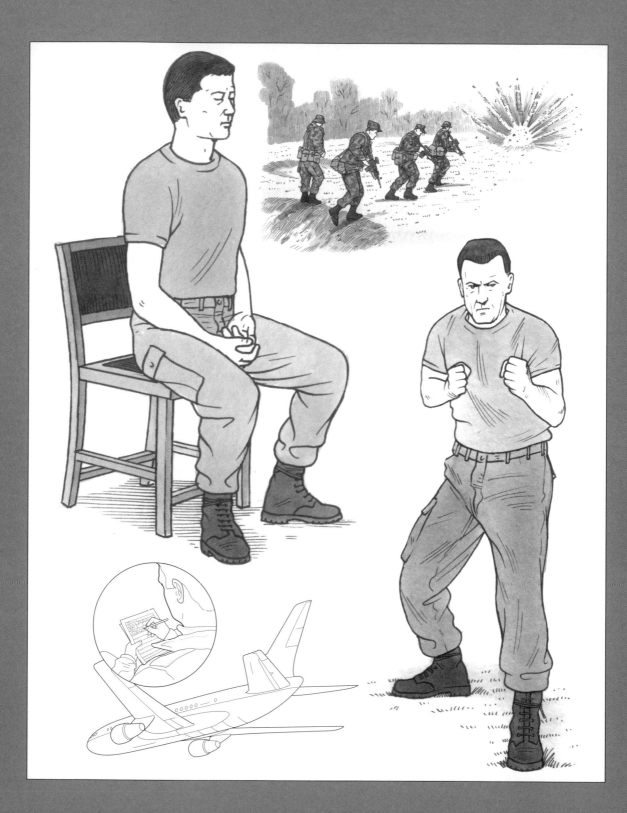

CHAPTER TWO

Handling Combat Stress

However hard the training, however tough the mind, few soldiers are totally immune to the trauma of combat. During battle, a soldier will experience sights, sounds and smells which are extreme and bewildering, and unlike anything encountered in civilian life. To function effectively, a soldier must quickly learn to cope with combat's mental pressures in the midst of battle.

Mutilation, the sudden death of friends and comrades, the almost animal noises of human beings in agony, the huge gas blast of artillery shells, personal injury – the range of sensations goes beyond almost anything encountered in civilian life.

Such experience takes its toll. Soldiers have likened combat to being in continual car accidents, or being part of the worst civil disaster imaginable, but actually participating in making it worse. For some, it is too much.

The shock of seeing death and chaos leaves them emotionally crippled. Unable to cope, their condition damages them as individuals and also detracts from the efficiency and morale of their unit. Detailed studies of 20th-century conflicts have shown that units experiencing sustained combat over several days suffer an average psychological casualty rate of one in every four soldiers. This rate climbs with every extra day of combat. Facing such a significant problem, military researchers have devoted huge amounts of time and money to finding ways of 'battleproofing' the soldier. This chapter will reveal their discoveries and also reflect on why elite special forces units have almost negligible levels of mental casualties as compared to regular units.

THE CHANGING FACE OF WAR

Although there is a modern label for adverse psychological reactions to combat – combat stress reaction (CSR) – combat has obviously always been traumatic. Yet the battlefield developed during the 20th century in such a way as to make mental damage a much greater likelihood.

The first development was mobility. The 20th century saw the true advent of mechanised warfare on land, on sea and in the air. Achievements in vehicular design during the 1930s led to the application of Blitzkrieg warfare by the Germans in 1939. Blitzkrieg placed a premium on violent and deep penetrations into enemy territory while maintaining effective communications between the various aircraft, armoured units and infantry squads involved. The effect was to create a highly fluid battlefield, constantly changing and uncertain. Rather than there being clear battle lines, opposing forces could be confusingly enmeshed to depths of hundreds of miles. A soldier involved in such combat therefore had to cope with the tremendous strain of not knowing his overall situation, frequently being surrounded by enemy forces and all the time trying to maintain efficient use of equipment, vehicles, communications and tactics. Facing or executing the Blitzkrieg warfare in World War II was thus psychologically exhausting. Some US divisions, for example, during the Tunisian battles of the Kasserine and Faid passes, actually had 35 per cent stress casualties out of their overall casualty figure, a figure no doubt heightened by the rawness of the US troops who were all experiencing their first battle. In other theatres, it was common for a division of men to lose 1600 soldiers to combat-related stress.

Since World War II, the trends of mobile warfare have continued expanding. Modern aircraft, vehicles and communications now have all-weather capabilities – capabilities which led to what is known as continuous warfare (CW). Continuous warfare was a doctrine that emerged during the Cold War. On both sides of the iron curtain, tacticians recognised that to be decisive, the tempo of warfare would have to be maintained night and day. For the soldier, this introduced some of the critical causes of CSR: sleep deprivation, low–light-level operations, increased fatigue through longer operational hours, operations in harsh weather, longer periods without rest or food, and isolation from one's colleagues because of the greater operating distances. The effect of CW can be seen in recent conflicts such as the Yom Kippur War in the Middle East in 1973, when some 30 per cent of Israeli casualties suffered during the war were psychiatric.

Another major change is technological. Modern weapons are perfect killing machines and the mutilation they inflict can be appalling to witness. A simple high-velocity bullet from an AKM assault rifle, for example, will tumble through the human body, tearing and shattering internal tissue, before exploding out the other side of the body and leaving a gaping, infected hole. Soldiers in the Vietnam War were often stunned when only two or three rounds from their M16 rifles would tear limbs off their opponents. Conversely, they had to handle the sickening experience of seeing friends physically annihilated by modern anti-personnel mines. For Iraqi soldiers in the Gulf War, artillery and air power had such enormous range, accuracy and destructive force that even rear areas became dangerous, and there was consequently no place in which the soldier felt safe or able to relax.

Defensive positions

Defensive positions provide confidence to face an attack, although studies show that soldiers tend to be less aggressive with their weapons when in dug outs and bunkers. The soldier needs to treat them as fighting positions and not as hiding positions.

The final change, also related to technology, is the intellectual demand of operations. Almost all soldiers in developed armies must now be accustomed to using highly advanced machinery. Tools such as satellite positioning systems, computerised artillery ranging devices, ground-to-air missile defences and coded communications require great concentration to use. In the heat of battle, this concentration is stretched to the absolute limit and the conflicting demands of preserving life while focusing on equipment operation prove a further drain on mental stamina.

All these factors of the modern battlefield create the perfect environment for breeding CSR, and we will turn to its symptoms and treatments in a moment. What is enlightening is that, among elite units such as the SAS, Green Berets, US Marine Corps, Royal Marine Commandos and so on, CSR is much more of a rarity than in regular units. This fact stands despite the fact that elite troops will frequently be placed in situations of greater stress than almost any other fighting man or woman. A telling example of this comes from World War II. During the 38-day period between 6 June and 13 July 1944, two units were compared for their percentage of stress casualties amongst their wounded in action (WIA). The elite 82nd Airborne Division was involved in horrendous fighting around

Fighting stance

In unarmed combat, adopting a strong physical posture actually leads the brain to generate greater confidence – the body actually leads the mind, not the other way around.

Normandy at this time and suffered an appalling 4196 WIA, yet stress casualties never exceeded 6 in every 100 casualties. By contrast, an infantry division in Italy endured 1800 WIA, but its level of stress victims was 13 to every 100 casualties – twice as high as the airborne unit. The figures are not just restricted to particular battles; the percentages of stress casualties remained at those levels for the rest of the war. Another telling figure was that the 442nd Regimental Combat Team, which recruited troops mainly from a Japanese background, but who lived in Hawaii, suffered almost no stress-related casualties in the entire Italian campaign. This was despite their being very highly decorated; it seems that their desire to prove their national commitment to the United States, despite their ancestry, created extraordinary levels of motivation (source of figures: US Army Research Institute).

So what separates the elite soldier from the regular soldier, the strong mind from the vulnerable one?

COMBAT STRESS REACTION

Combat stress reaction (CSR) covers a multitude of psychological conditions. For the purposes of definition, we can say that it is a mental state induced by combat which impairs an individual's emotional, intellectual and physical ability to function as a soldier. CSR is different from mental injuries or instabilities which result from physical injuries. Constant exposure to artillery fire can disrupt the inner ear through a constant pounding from rapid changes in air pressure, the result being physical shakiness and a confused mental condition – what was in part termed 'shell shock' during the first half of the 20th century. Similarly, blood loss or oxygen deprivation during battle will profoundly alter the casualty's mental state, with symptoms including confusion, aggression and inability to concentrate.

By contrast, CSR is a purely mental condition, born out of the response to witnessing and participating in combat. The symptoms vary considerably between individuals, but the following list is typical:

- **Aggression/irritability** - The casualty experiences uncontrollable aggression which is not only directed at the enemy, but also at those around him and inanimate objects. This aggression can be hair trigger and need only minor incidents (such as loud noises) to activate it.
- **Alcohol/drugs** - The casualty's alcohol/drug intake may increase dramatically as he attempts to shut out traumatic memories. In actual fact, the taking of drugs in whatever form usually aggravates his depression and anxiety.
- **Anxiety** - Not just simple worry, anxiety is an abiding and obsessive tension which dramatically affects the person's ability to sleep, think and control his behaviour. Symptoms often include a physical jumpiness.
- **Apathy** - The combat-shocked soldier may mentally withdraw from the outside world and show little interest in the events or situations around him.
- **Body temperature variations** - Alternation between feeling hot and sweaty, and chilly is common and often bears no relation to the outside temperature or climate.
- **Bowel/bladder problems** - Particularly during the build-up and the battle itself, a soldier may lose the ability to control the bowel and bladder muscles. Urination may become involuntary and the soldier will have bouts of diarrhoea. The frequency of urination is also greatly increased.
- **Catatonia** - A CSR casualty can physically freeze and be unable to move his limbs, even under extreme coercion.
- **Concentration deficit** - The CSR casualty is unable to hold his attention on one subject or object for very long and thus is not capable of rational thought.
- **Depression** - Chronic depression often accompanies CSR and features a deep sense of self-criticism, an acute pessimism, fear of the future and fatigue.
- **Eating/drinking disorders** - The casualty becomes uninterested in food or drink, resulting in weight loss, fatigue and illness.
- **Fatigue** - Fatigue is normal after long hours spent in combat, but CSR victims can often exhibit chronic fatigue even after adequate rest.
- **Memory loss** - Even short-term memory is lost under acute stress; the combatant may have a general inability to remember orders even when given only moments ago.
- **Mood swings** - Mood alters constantly and ranges from deep depression to strange moments of elation.
- **Nausea/vomiting** - The soldier may experience attacks of nausea and vomiting, even when the danger has passed. Eating can often be difficult because involuntary 'heaves' accompany the swallowing of food.
- **Obsessive activities** - The casualty undertakes repetitious actions to no purpose, such as field stripping and assembling his weapon beyond normal maintenance requirements or obsessive talking about a single subject.
- **Recklessness** - The soldier may display a disregard for the safety of himself and others in his actions.
- **Self-loathing** - The soldier may feel a sense of deep personal unworthiness and constantly make unfavourable comparisons with others.
- **Speech disorder** - The casualty may suffer a breakdown in communication skills, with pronunciation becoming slurred and unintelligibility increasing.

Effects of altitude on marksmanship

At high altitudes, marksman-ship deteriorates by nearly 50 per cent and takes up to two weeks of acclimatisation to regain its sea-level standards of performance.

Sea level

High altitude

soldier's capacity to function as part of a military unit. Furthermore, entire units can suffer from group symptoms as a whole. These can include: high rates of desertion and AWOL (absent without leave); disintegration of unit cohesion; lack of discipline; defiance of officers' orders; tasks left undone or completed slowly; general deterioration in appearance; infighting; open disrespect of unit routines and traditions; low morale; and complaints. Another common symptom is a high degree of sickness reported – usually minor illnesses such as headaches, stomach pains or flu – especially prior to combat. Indeed, medical officers are trained to expect a sudden rush of minor ailments to be treated prior to any action and also to expect the highest percentage of CSR patients to arrive for treatment during the first few days of combat breaking out.

We have already touched on the overall context of modern warfare in which CSR occurs. Yet there is also a more specific range of reasons for CSR and it is these which form the focus for the conditioning training of the elite forces.

- **Trembling** – The hands in particular may shake, but this can extend to whole-body trembling.
- **Withdrawal from reality** – Overwhelmed by the world around him, the soldier might suddenly withdraw into himself and either succumb to complete inertia or inhabit an imaginary or hallucinatory world.

A glance at all these symptoms makes it obvious that combat stress can destroy the

THE LIMITS OF ENDURANCE

Although many things can trigger combat stress, there is a certain range of conditions which are more responsible for this than others. A central pillar of combat stress is sleep deprivation. Disruption of the body's natural sleep rhythms, particularly between the hours of 0200 and 0600 when sleep is usually at its deepest, significantly affects the soldier's ability to think and operate. Studies in both the United States and United Kingdom showed that, if sleeplessness is maintained for more than 48 hours, then a military unit will almost totally cease to function and the soldiers will start to display psychological disorders. Even auditory and visual hallucinations occurred. Particularly affected were the soldiers' decision-making skills and memory, and they became more susceptible to fear and anxiety (interestingly, weapons maintenance and map plotting were not affected). The problem with sleep deprivation is the disruption of the body's natural rhythms and it is compounded by travel, especially when a soldier crosses time zones during transport flights. Sleep-deprivation stress is often exacerbated by having to operate in low-light conditions. Working in the dark has the simple effect of making the soldier more susceptible to his imagination, as fears are projected into the blackness rather than being actually seen and understood. This type of problem is particularly acute for special forces soldiers, who undertake many of their operations during the cover of night.

Another major factor in CSR development is, unsurprisingly, the weapons that the soldier has arraigned against him. Investigation into the psychological impact of weaponry was begun in World War I, when whole new categories of weaponry entered the fray, with a deplorable increase in levels of mortality. World War II continued the research. Work conducted in North Africa threw up a fascinating spectrum of results, including which weapons men feared the most and how they adjusted to those weapons over a period of time. The weapons judged 'most frightening' by 97 per cent of 120 psychiatric casualties were those used in various types of shellfire and bombing. At the point of first contact, air attack was the most alarming according to 50 per cent of those involved; artillery fire was nominated by 20 per cent. Yet, only 11 days into battle, those priorities had switched entirely as the soldiers became more familiar with the actual results of the weapons deployed against them (artillery was accurate and destructive, whereas dive bombing was noisy, but generally ineffective). Further studies into the reasons why men feared weapons tended to show that

Stress testing

A controversial stress testing device used by US military research groups was to get soldiers to fill in complicated life-assurance forms while flying aboard a plane which they believed was about to crash land.

accuracy, rapidity of fire and volume of noise were the primary sources of anxiety.

Fear of weapons induces a central cause of CSR in soldiers – death anxiety. As the term suggests, this is quite simply the fear of death. An individual concerned about his mortality is under the constant stress of predicting the nature, time and experience of his demise. As we would expect, this problem increases with the duration in combat. During World War II, almost any soldier who was engaged in heavy fighting on a daily basis was rendered mentally unstable after about five to 10 days of action, depending on how effectively his basic needs (food, sleep etc.) had been catered for.

BATTLEPROOFING

Having looked at what combat can do to the mind, we now turn towards the techniques of avoiding, or at least mitigating, combat stress. The elite forces act as our guides in this.

Special forces, as already noted, have a much lower incidence of mental difficulties than regular troops. Yet elite-unit operations would, on the surface of things, seem to have some of the most stress-inducing conditions that combatants can face. The operations tend to have a disproportionately high risk of death and failure. Units are small and, once operational, tend to be isolated from the protective umbrella of the general might of the armed forces. Many special operations soldiers work entirely alone, coping with stress without a sympathetic ear and also handling the intense boredom of long vigils. The physical strains are likewise enormous, with pack weights reaching up to 54.5kg (120lb) in weight on some operations (such as those conducted by the SAS in the Gulf War which required the soldiers to be self-sufficient for a period of time) and sleep deprivation being a persistent drain on energy and motivation. And yet their resilience nonetheless is legendary.

Top reasons why men fear weapons – World War II study

Conventional bomber – Accuracy

Dive bombers – Noise

Mortars – Accuracy

Machine guns – Rapid fire

Artillery – Accuracy

Adjusting to artillery

The soldier must have experience of close artillery fire in training, otherwise the sensations of blast and noise will leave him unsettled and confused in combat.

So, why do special operations soldiers endure where so many ordinary soldiers would succumb? Naturally, details are hard to come by, as the special forces are secretive about all aspects of their advanced training. Yet details of their methods are steadily becoming more available, if only for the fact that elite forces expertise tends to filter itself out towards other more regular units, such as the US and Royal Marines, which exercise elite capabilities, but are less concealed.

Of central significance to producing soldiers resilient to the traumas of combat is the process of 'battleproofing' or 'battle inoculation'. Battleproofing is based on making the mind 'familiar' with the experience of combat through realistic training. The human mind is effectively like an enormous filing system. When a person comes upon a new experience, that experience is tested against the files of memory to find an experience which was similar in the past which can

guide future actions. Depending on the relevance of the match, the individual is able to make a judgement and respond to the situation. If there is little previous experience to guide in a particular situation, the brain finds the nearest equivalent and then makes a new 'file' based on what happens. The problem with combat is that, because it is so extreme by nature, unless you have actually experienced it, there is almost no way to prepare for it. This is where battleproofing comes in. The essence of battleproofing is to generate as much realism in the training scenarios as possible, thus taking away the shock factor of actual combat.

So how is this accomplished? A good example can be taken from SAS counter-terrorist training. During hostage-rescue exercises, SAS soldiers use a specially constructed sequence of rooms known as the 'killing house', in which a hostage, usually an SAS colleague, is positioned surrounded by

Coping with confinement

Armoured crews are especially vulnerable to combat stress because of the cramped, hot conditions in which they work. In battle these conditions often lead to fears of fire and being trapped, and communications with other units must be maintained to avoid feeling isolated.

life-size cut-out figures of his terrorist captors. With incredible speed, an SAS team then makes an explosive entry using stun grenades – grenades which impart a huge flash and bang, but which have almost no lethality. The noise and the smoke are intense and the room is plunged into darkness. In this confusion, the entry team target the terrorists with their laser sights and then take them out using live ammunition, often firing bullets only inches from the prisoner's head. With all the terrorists dead, the prisoner is snatched and dragged out of the room at lightning speed.

The training exercise must be exercised with real aggression and it is repeated over and over again until the demands of the action become almost second nature. It battleproofs the soldiers on several levels. First, the use of live ammunition helps the soldiers become accustomed to the actual sounds and sensation their firearms have when being fired in earnest in a certain physical space. Secondly, the fact that there is a live person within the firing range makes the soldier accept the responsibility of his actions. Thirdly, the person who is acting as the hostage is himself trained by becoming used to the noise of bullets hissing past him while remaining composed and alert. It is the final stage, however, the constant repetition of the training, which is perhaps most important. Repeating the exercise over and over again allows the sensations of the shooting, smoke and impact of rounds and the mental processes of lightning-fast decision-making to enter the 'files' of the familiar. Thus, were the soldier actually to go into real combat, the brain would not be as traumatised by the sensations as that of someone not trained by these methods.

LIVE EXERCISES

Battleproofing exercises of this type are practised by elite forces around the world

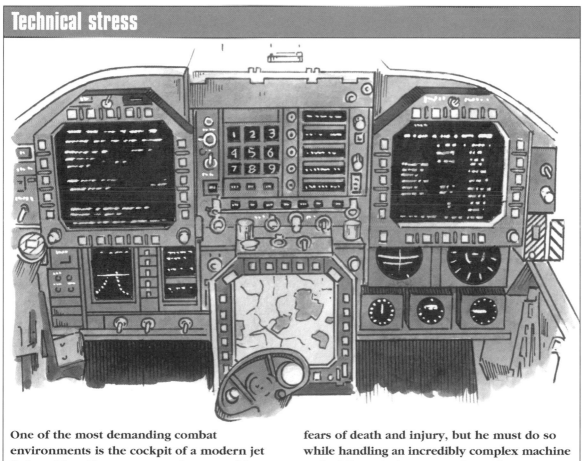

Technical stress

One of the most demanding combat environments is the cockpit of a modern jet fighter. The pilot must not only cope with fears of death and injury, but he must do so while handling an incredibly complex machine and while enduring nauseating G-forces.

and have become more of a presence in regular units. The US Marine Corps, for instance, has huge combined arms exercises in which live ordnance is fired from artillery and dropped from aircraft so that soldiers become accustomed to the huge percussions. Iraqi soldiers undergo training in which they crawl under barbed wire while instructors fire live rounds into the ground literally inches from their heads. Recently, more insidious training methods have come to light. US Special Forces soldiers, around the time of the Vietnam War, underwent special training in which they were sat in front of a TV monitor which reeled off horrific and distressing images for hour after hour. The viewing individual eventually became desensitised to watching human suffering and so, it was assumed, would be less susceptible to the trauma of actual violence. The effectiveness of this technique is actually questionable, for, although the subject becomes acclimatised to the two-dimensional violence of the screen, this actually has little sensory correspondence with the three-dimensional world. However, part of current US Marine officer training is to send the officer candidates to the trauma ward of a major hospital for several days. Here, they become used to the sight of serious injuries and sudden death in a way that battleproofs them for the sight, sound and smell of casualties in a war zone (they are usually sent to a hospital in a large city, such as Washington, where they can expect a high number of gunshot wounds). In a similar manner, special forces instructors in Ecuador use real corpses as training aids when teaching recruits about anatomy for combat purposes.

NEED FOR REALISM

The key to battleproofing training is to make it as close to the experience of real combat as possible, replicating its brutality, pressure and sensations with close attention to detail. Such training should also build the exceptional physical stamina required by modern soldiers, for physical durability tends to guard against mental fragility. Elite units tend to have the financial resources to invest very heavily in training and to be able to use copious amounts of live ammunition, thus their battleproofing has been seen to be especially effective. Furthermore, elite units tend to have each individual in possession of the full range of information about the nature of their mission. Unlike regular units, where there is sometimes an information deficit amongst the lower ranks, elite squads will usually have undergone full and complex rehearsals of what is operationally required. This in itself reduces the likelihood of CSR, as the soldier has a clear understanding of what is needed to survive in combat.

Military training should not only bring about a familiarity with fighting, but it

Stress testing exercise – US 1950s

Pick out the Cs from the Os. Keep the eye moving quickly; if your attention wanders, go back to the beginning and start again. Are you composed or increasingly frustrated?

COOOOOOOCOOOCOOOCOOCOCOCOCOCOCOCOCOCOCOCOCOC
COCOCOCOCOCOCOCOCOCOCOCOCOCOCOCOOOCOCOOOCOCOCO
OOOCOOOCOOCOOOOCOCCOOOOOCOOOOOOOCOOOOOCO

should also impart confidence in self and unit. Instilling confidence is vital to the prevention of adverse stress because the confident soldier is far less likely to suffer from the sense of helplessness than can come from being separated from the unit or cut off from the flow of information from the rear. Confidence must be built around several themes. First, there is confidence in decision-making skills. Elite units are trained so that if the leader of a unit is killed or put out of action, all others are sufficiently trained in decision-making so as to be able to step into their shoes immediately. The US Marine Corps also uses this philosophy. Following extensive research into the vital leadership role of NCOs in World War II, all Marine recruits are now placed in intensive

decision-making environments from the moment they arrive at training camp.

Confidence should also exist in weapons handling. British SAS and US Navy SEALs training involves recruits becoming familiar in handling almost every significant firearm used by the world's armies. This enables them to have a complete command of the tools of their trade and thus there are no gaps in competence which might prey on the soldier's mind. The confidence in weapons handling, however, is a two-way street. Elite units tend to hand-pick their weapons for reliability and firepower, so that they have little fear of being let down by their weapons at crucial moments. This is why the SAS have rejected use of the problematic British Army SA80 – which tends to

Effects of altitude

At 4572m (15,000ft) soldiers were found to suffer from chronic fatigue, problems with short- and long-term memory, lack of concentration and mood swings.

Hypnosis 1 – sitting position

Self-hypnosis begins by focusing on the slow rise and fall of the breath, while simultaneously relaxing the body, working from the toes to the top of the scalp.

suffer from alarming mechanical failures, such as the magazine suddenly dropping out – in preference of battle-tested weaponry such as the US M16A2 and the older L1A1 self-loading rifle.

Confidence also derives from unit support. Elite forces train in small, tightly knit groups, the members of which come to know one another intimately and which have an implicit trust in one another. In combat, this trust translates into motivation. Among soldiers motivation tends to come not from great ideals, though these are important, but from the desire not to fail one's comrades and not to let down the regimental name. Once soldiers have been through the shared exhaustions and demands of training, they tend to become highly motivated by their desire to protect and enhance the group. Once motivation is present to a high degree, CSR is less able to set in as the soldier keeps more of an outward-looking perspective towards his or her comrades-in-arms, rather than an introspection.

The role of the leaders also comes into play. They can be vital in motivating, or demotivating, the individual and the unit as a whole. Leadership qualities are explored in detail later. In terms of controlling combat stress by building up team and individual confidence, the leader's primary roles are, according to the US Army Research Institute, to:

- set realistic goals for the progressive development of individual, team and unit competence;
- systematically test the achievement of these goals;
- praise improvement and coach units towards achieving higher competence;
- single out individuals and teams for recognition and develop a spirit of accomplishment;
- point out reasons for confidence at every opportunity;
- present realistic and detailed expectations about future combat conditions;
- point out that the enemy faces the same conditions;
- develop in each soldier confidence in self, equipment, unit, training and leadership.

This list of confidence-building objectives is designed not only to give soldiers belief in their own abilities, but also to enable them to accept that they are being competently led and that their lives are in the hands of someone who knows what he is doing.

It is also up to the leader to look after the welfare of his men. Sleep and food delivery should be high on his list of priorities, for reasons we have already noted. Sleep breaks should be scheduled by the leader for whenever possible, and this includes elite units who need to keep their decision-making abilities fresher than most. If regular and lengthy periods of sleep are not possible, sleep research for the US Army has shown that some of the wearing effects of sleep deprivation can be offset by a simple 20–30-minute nap with a similar period for wake-up before an action is to take place. If the soldier can train himself to sleep in these circumstances, his energy levels will temporarily restore themselves just as he is going into action and he will become less susceptible to fatigue-related CSR.

Through battleproofing, confidence building, group motivation and good leadership, a soldier is far less likely to become a psychiatric casualty of war than those who have not benefited from such training. Yet battle is still a shocking experience to even those who have been recipients of the most rigorous training.

Hypnosis 2 – prone position

The soldier visualises the situation he fears, seeing himself performing confidently and boldly. The 'waking' brain will use the scenario as a model for future conduct.

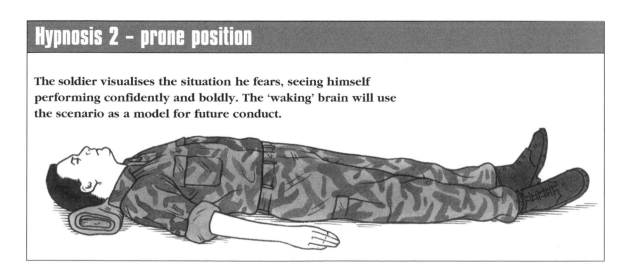

COPING WITH CHAOS

Even when CSR has set in, it is not irreversible. There is a body of recommended techniques which are designed to stop the progression of the condition and ultimately restore the casualty to some level of normality. The processes of professional psychiatric treatment of advanced CSR are scientifically and pharmaceutically complex, and are rather beyond the scope of this book. However, what has been deemed vital is that the casualty has the chance to air his anxiety to someone able to listen without judgement. In military terminology, this is known as 'ventilation'. The important factor of ventilation support is that the casualty is speaking to someone with genuine listening skills. This means that the listener does not interrupt the flow of speech unless there is a natural pause and then only to say something helpful. The listener should encourage the talker to pour out all his anxieties and must never indicate signs of boredom or lack of interest. By articulating most of his troubles, the traumatised soldier can share them in a wider context and thus see himself less as an isolated sufferer.

For more severe cases of CSR occurring suddenly on the battlefield, the 'crisis management' technique is the one advocated by the US Army Research Institute. The first stage of crisis management is to calm the distressed soldier as much as possible. This should be through a gentle but firm voice, clear commands and the enlistment of others who may be better placed to control the outburst. Secondly, the soldier should be protected from danger, either from himself or from putting himself in a vulnerable position. This, if necessary, can involve physical restraint. Thirdly, the officer or man who is dealing with the crisis must gather enough information to assess the cause of the CSR and judge what the best mode of action will be. If, for example, the soldier has just witnessed the violent death of a friend, he is

talking incoherently and seems to have lost the ability to listen to even simple instructions, he is a danger to himself and others, and evacuation is the best course.

Human support is the frontline of CSR care. However, there is also a series of physical relaxation techniques which, during the phase of pre- or post-battle, can go some way towards helping a soldier cope with trauma. Central amongst these relaxation techniques are those of breathing and self-hypnosis. Although such techniques may have a somewhat New Age stigma attached to them, in some military units around the world they are nonetheless now slowly gaining a wider currency. The US Army Research Institute recommends using breathing and self-suggestion techniques as part of regular military stress-control measures. and units such as the SEALs also have been known to use relaxation techniques as a regular part of their aikido martial arts training.

BENEFITS OF MEDITATION

The actual techniques of breathing-based meditation and self-suggestion are described in the diagrams here in this chapter, but the benefits of the techniques are clear.

Meditation allows the heartbeat to slow down as well as the blood pressure to drop, and this reduces the physical symptoms of anxiety, which in turn leads the mind to feel more balanced and restored. Also, it allows the soldier to perform his own form of internal battleproofing. This is done by the soldier imagining himself coping with situations about which he is fearful during the process of meditation. The human mind is remarkable in that its 'filing system' cannot actually tell the difference between events that are vividly imagined and those that are actually experienced. Thus, a soldier who is particularly afraid of artillery fire can, to some measure, 'inoculate' himself against CSR by visualising himself in the midst of a

Environmental stress

The physical environment adds to the soldier's mental state. Four negative elements are cold, heat, altitude and wetness; all can lead to lack of concentration and change of mood.

barrage being calm, alert and focused on his objectives. Likewise, a special forces soldier can mentally rehearse a mission in order to give himself a clear sense of what he is doing when he does actually go into the arena of combat. Of course, the technique is not a substitute for the physical experience itself, but it can go some way to helping a soldier control and prevent CSR, without initially exposing himself to danger.

At the end of the day, however, perhaps the only surefire way of resisting adverse reactions to combat experience is to go through the experience itself and come out on the other side.

Battle can break or harden the soldier, but if the chaos of battle is managed with some degree of confidence, then that confidence will be taken forward into the next encounter.

Of course, underlying this chapter is the harsh fact that human beings do not have infinite tolerance for sights of horror and death. The realities of combat will forever leave their psychological mark on those who have to face them.

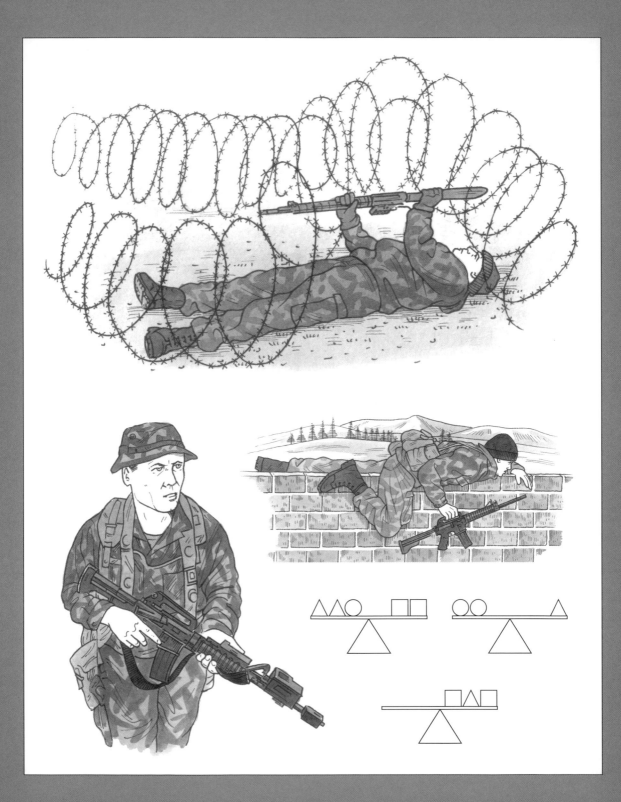

CHAPTER THREE

Recruitment and Training

The 20th century saw an increasing professionalisation of the world's military forces, particularly following the technological and tactical revelations of the German Blitzkrieg in 1939 and 1940. The success of the German Army against superior numbers proved that the more professional the soldier, the more chance he or she has of achieving success.

At the opening of World War II, the Allies expected a repetition of the defensive stalemate of World War I. Yet, when only seven German armoured and motorised divisions punched through the Low Countries and achieved the capitulation of France between 10 May and 19 June (little more than five weeks), the world awoke to a new military reality. The German forces had used excellence of training, a strong application of new technology, modern communications and disdain for old styles of warfare to produce a combat style which overwhelmed now-outdated defensive strategies.

The Allies did catch up, but a profound change had now occurred within the structure and function of armies. The lesson of World War I – that sheer manpower could be dominated by sheer firepower – reached its peak in World War II. What the military establishment of all nations now required was not only men and women of courage, but also individuals who could apply themselves with great intelligence to a mobile, technically governed battlefield.

Following the Vietnam War (1963–75), more of the world's armies realised that a non-professional, conscripted army was, in many cases, a political liability and also a military drain. Weapons technology and the need for quick, decisive military solutions has led to armies reducing the numbers of personnel, but investing more in their training and professionalism. Concurrently, the continuing rise of 'low-intensity' and 'guerrilla' warfare since 1945 means that armies must have specialists who can deal with situations alternating between high-impact combat and humanitarian care, a switch most ordinary soldiers are unable to handle.

As a result, recruitment and training in armed forces has become more specialised. Recruiters now look for individuals to make a definite contribution of character and skills, rather than just fill out quotas. Nowhere is this truer than in the elite forces. There can be no such thing as a 'weak link' in a special forces team. Each element of the whole must function with confidence and tactical aplomb. Standards must be rigorously applied to every elite soldier, making the recruitment and training processes for these squads the hardest in world, far beyond the capabilities of most individuals. This chapter is about choosing and creating an elite soldier. Our focus here is on what qualities of mind a recruiter looks for when selecting personnel for an elite unit, and also what mental abilities the soldier must develop and demonstrate during his harsh training.

SELECTING THE ELITE

The irony of selecting military personnel is that the higher you go up the ladder of expertise, the more subjective the selection process becomes. Many members of elite regiments come from existing military backgrounds – the SAS, for instance, tends to use the Royal Marines and the Parachute Regiment as its recruiting grounds – so the recruiters already know that the individual has good basic military skills. This is not always the case, however, and many elite units (especially those of a larger scale, such as marines) do take in raw recruits. Whatever their background, what the recruiters are looking for is that extra depth of personality and intelligence, which can only be judged by putting the would-be soldier through severe physical and mental challenges over a prolonged period.

We shall turn to that process shortly; however, before any soldier can enter an elite force, their mental profile is effectively screened through a battery of tests and questions. A would-be US Marine, for example, has to pay a visit to the US Marine Corps office recruiter before he or she gets anywhere near a training camp. The US Marine Corps distinguishes itself from the US Army by promising membership of a close brotherhood of elite troops more akin to a religious order than a military unit. Yet the reward for this acute sense of belonging – which will last the recruit's entire life – is nothing more than the promise of hardship, toil, adversity and pain. The recruiter's job is to see whether the young person before him is up to that challenge.

Naturally, a first level of screening consists of a physical assessment. This generally focuses on illnesses or problems such as unacceptably defective vision, epilepsy or asthma, or sexually transmitted diseases such as hepatitis or HIV. Physical problems are an easily identified source of rejection. More complex is the recruiter's assessment of the candidate's character and background. Marine recruiters will probe deeply into the applicant's background to find moments of courage, determination or leadership which may indicate performance as a future US Marine. If the individual struggled through poverty to gain qualifications or support a

Intelligence Tests

Intelligence Test 1

Three white and three black blocks are shown separated by spaces. Can you completely reverse their position by moving one block at a time to an adjacent position or by jumping over an adjacent block or space?

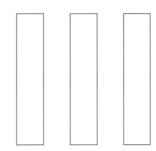

Intelligence Test 2

Which shape should be used to fill in the blank space?

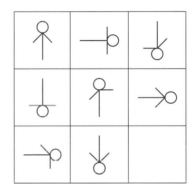

Intelligence Test 3

First, work out the numerical values of the triangle, circle and square shapes on the see-saw. Once you have this, which collection of shapes (A, B or C) should be used to balance the last see-saw?

family, then such might indicate strength of mind. If the person has captained sports teams, this shows that he or she can take responsibility for his or her actions when these affect others. There are no hard and fast rules about what questions the recruiters should ask, but, as experienced selectors and long-standing US Marines, they become adept at picking out those with promise. They are equally adept at defining those whose characters are flawed or who will suffer from mental problems. Criminal records usually constitute a complete barrier to entering the US Marine Corps – a respect for society and people is a prerequisite – whereas those who have dependants are often rejected because of the problems which arise over supporting a family on a meagre military wage.

Gradually, the recruiter will build up a profile of the candidate and form a judgement as to whether he or she is suitable to

Training realism

Training for combat must be as realistic as possible. If carried out in this way, then the shock of actual fighting is reduced during the actual experience. Here a soldier is pictured undergoing an accurate simulation of mine-field clearance.

be a US Marine. Although the person may have a strong character, he or she also has to display the another mental quality demanded by all military elites – intelligence. All entrants to any branch of the US military forces take the Armed Services Vocational Aptitude Battery (ASVAB) tests. These test all aspects of mental dexterity; however, whereas some US units take personnel with scores of as low as 21, the US Marine Corps will not accept candidates with a score of below 31 (actually, two-thirds of US Marines have scores of more than 50).

The exacting standards applied by the US Marine Corps are typical of the world's elite forces. The US Marines' British equivalent, the Royal Marines, generally require a good academic background and competence in both mathematics and English – both will be required in tactical manoeuvres and communications. The Royal Marines does not, however, confuse academic achievement with actual intelligence, and it looks for recruits who can demonstrate mental ability in situations of stress and difficulty. The selection criteria of more secretive units are less easily identified. Initial selection for units such as the SAS, Green Berets, US Marine Force Reconn and Russian Spetsnaz is often conducted by a trained psychologist, who will open up highly personal issues with the candidate and make very critical observations to see how the candidate reacts to stress. If the soldier is to go on to special duties – such as undercover work – his or her abilities with foreign languages will be tested and approved. During World War II, agents being recruited for the British Special Operations Executive (SOE) would find the recruiter slipping continually into French or German to see if the candidate hesitated or became lost. Any sign that the soldier lacked total comprehension of these vital undercover languages would lead to his being dropped.

A final measure for the special forces recruiter is to test the candidate's discretion.

Many elite units conduct work of the utmost secrecy, a situation often at odds with the unit's glamorous status in the public mind. Individuals who thrive on public recognition often make bad special forces soldiers and cannot be trusted to maintain official secrets. After the globally visible action by the SAS during the Iranian Embassy siege, the SAS training camp at Hereford was besieged by gangs of young men marching outside the camp gates in an attempt to join up. As the attempt to enlist was in most cases prompted by the desire to share in the 'hard man' public image of the SAS, almost all were entirely unsuitable (most were dispatched by making them run continuously around a track until they collapsed and were sent home). Units such as the SAS tend to look for individuals who are very mentally self-sufficient and have no need for public notoriety. Because the human drive for status is very strong, these individuals are quite rare. The maxim of organisations such as the Israeli Sayeret Mat'kal – that all is well as long as its operations do not make the headlines – is only true because of the exceptional levels of self-restraint shown by its officers and men.

Yet, while the elite forces require people who are emotionally stable, they do not want people who tend to be passive. Elite forces' missions tend to require unusual levels of aggressive commitment. Special forces soldiers have to have the flexibility to see all sides of a problem, but they also have to be able to pursue a military goal with a single-minded vigour. This is the quality known as 'mental endurance' and it is this which is tested during training.

TEACHING TO SURVIVE

Fighting is actually not one of the most natural human pursuits. A study conducted by Colonel S. L. A. Marshal during World War II found that, in battle, only about 15 per cent of combat troops actually found the presence of mind to fire their weapons at the

45

enemy. The remainder were paralysed or confused about the events around them and simply clutched their weapons. This did not just apply to 'green' units of new recruits; even supposedly battle-hardened squads showed the same tendency. Marshall analysed a particular battle on Makin Island in the Pacific, in which a charge by Japanese troops against positions of the US 165th Infantry Regiment was resisted by only 36 men actually firing back. This accounts for the fact that all the US soldiers in the forward positions were killed, even though their weaponry was more than a match for the Japanese bayonets and swords.

The conclusion of Marshall's report was that, in general, men only actively fight in a battle if the sheer weight of circumstances compels them to do so or if their officers force them into action. This latter fact places an incredible burden on leadership – Lieutenant Colonel Robert G. Cole of the 502nd Parachute Regiment fighting at the Carentan Causeway in 1944 found that he had to walk up and down his lines bullying each man into using his weapon.

The reasons for this are complex and are well explored in Joanna Bourke's book *An Intimate History of Killing* (London: Granta; 1999). Central amongst these reasons is the effect that long-distance weaponry has on the mind of the soldier. If killing can be accomplished at a significant distance from the soldier – with some weapons, the enemy does not have to be even seen – the enemy can start to seem 'unreal', despite the presence of bullets and explosions. For the elite soldier, the situation is somewhat different. Special forces operations tend to achieve a violent intimacy with the enemy, closing on him in the claustrophobic confines of a building, jungle or hijacked aircraft. Chris Ryan, the former SAS soldier who served in the Gulf War, has recounted how he had to break the neck of an Iraqi soldier with his bare arms when his presence was detected.

Elite missions, by their covert nature, often bring the soldier into very close contact with the enemy and sometimes demand the silent or rapid killing of people at close quarters. So how is this violent instinct instilled and mixed with the ability to survive all manner of adversity and still prosecute a mission with intelligence and commitment?

The secret, as ever, lies in the intensity and realism of the training. Training serves either to instil skills or to refresh them. For those giving the training, it is the arena in which they judge whether someone is suitable for service in an elite regiment. Training tends to fall into two different types. First is the basic level of training which builds up the soldier's (or candidate's) levels of mental fitness and also tests their ability to reason under pressure. This stage is mainly a testing of character and personal endurance. The second is the training in specific military skills: firearms technique, demolitions, surveillance, communications etc. In this, the soldier is turned from a fit, stable individual into a military specialist. We shall look at each of these training levels in turn and see what mental characteristics are required to survive and excel in them, and which attitudes and behaviours are looked for.

BASIC TRAINING

For the elite soldier, there is no such thing as 'basic' training. Induction into an elite unit requires the soldier to undergo some of the most punishing physical exertion the human frame is capable of enduring. Basic training can last for anything up to 40 weeks and, during that time, the candidate is assessed on many different criteria. From a psychological point of view, the trainers are looking for:

● **Tenacity.** Can the soldier maintain his commitment to succeed even when he is physically and mentally at the limits of his endurance? This tendency is primarily tested through seeing how the character

The Killing House

The Killing House tests SAS soldiers for the ability to make quick-fire decisions in chaotic and unpredictable situations filled with noise, smoke and confusion. Instructors look for clarity in action and maintaining a ruthless combat tempo.

holds up to exhausting marches and physical tasks.

- **Innovation and intelligence.** Does the soldier demonstrate distinctive methods of problem-solving under pressure and are his thought processes clear even under times of acute stress? Clear thinking is hampered by exhaustion, so

the elite forces push the limits of each soldier's physical endurance and then see if he is still capable of making tactical and practical decisions.

- **Team spirit.** Although there is a place for isolationists in the elite forces, most special forces training looks for people who will actively look towards the

Target minimisation

Even in the simple act of crossing a wall, the soldier must be trained to make himself as small a target as possible, imagining himself from the enemy's point of view. Failure to do this should be penalised in training to give the exercise consequence.

welfare of the group and put their own interests second. Team players will also tend to make better tacticians because they accept that others have talents which they do not possess.

- **Self-control.** Soldiers should show a solid control over their emotions. Elite troops are often called upon to make split-second decisions, the consequence of which is that someone lives or dies. Any sign that an individual is predisposed towards psychotic violence brings almost immediate dismissal – studies have shown that excessively violent personalities cannot adapt to discipline, are egocentric and boastful, and also tend to crumple during times of real danger.

- **Sense of humour.** A sense of humour is not just welcome, but essential. Studies conducted during the Korean War found that soldiers with a sense of humour (particularly a dry, cynical type) tended to make better fighters.

Each individual trainer adds to this list his own set of criteria and his own tests to bring out the soldier's true character. The initial training period is designed to be as punishing and demanding as possible. Although people can hide their true character for a short time, in hard, prolonged training, an individual will not have enough stamina to maintain this. To give us an idea of the mental demands a soldier faces during basic training, we will look in detail at the initial training course for entry into the SAS.

SAS Basic Training
The SAS training regimen is justifiably claimed as amongst the very hardest, if not

the hardest, of all military training programmes. Those who want to join the SAS can usually gain a 'taster' of the actual training by attending the Special Forces Briefing Course (SFBC) held at SAS HQ at Hereford. This is a weekend course which forms an introductory test of the candidate's mental and physical stamina, and gives the candidate a chance to discover whether the SAS is for him. The course lasts three days (usually from Friday to Sunday). On Friday, the candidate undergoes a series of mental tests relating to military practice. These include tests in comprehending and handling maps, IQ and first aid tests, and assessment of levels of military knowledge. Almost all of the rest of the weekend is devoted to physical testing. Saturday usually consists of two runs: two miles (3.2km) in 18 minutes and eight miles (12.9km) in 1 hour 40 minutes. Sunday involves runs of about 1.5 hours in length, but this time the students have to carry a colleague for most of the period.

The physical aspects of the SFBC are interspersed with briefings and seminars on the traditions and lifestyle of the SAS. Although this is only the very first step on the ladder to becoming an SAS soldier, the trainers are still watching the candidates extremely closely for their mental qualities. In particular, they look for someone who:

- responds quickly and without procrastination to commands;
- does not attempt to show off or catch attention;
- shows the ability not only to complete the physical tests, but also to prove the spirit of effort by trying to maintain a place in the lead group;

Adaptive thinking 1

A soldier should be able to adapt whatever he has to hand to a new purpose. This 'adaptive thinking' gives a good indicator of the soldier's tactical acumen.

- demonstrates the self-awareness to make his own decisions and not merely follow the will of the group;
- shows that his physical skills are matched by his intelligence and judgement, something especially important in navigation exercises.

If the trainers are satisfied that the person meets these requirements, they can proceed to the selection phase of basic training. This is known as Route Selection and much of it takes place in the Brecon Beacons in Wales. Although the mountains in the Brecon Beacons are not particularly high, during winter they are very inhospitable, with high winds, fog and freezing sleet making hypothermia a real possibility. For around 18 days, the recruits are put through a series of increasingly harsh survival marches. The pace is relentless. Each day, the recruit finds himself either struggling up mountain sides with 22.6kg (50lb) of Bergen pack strapped to his back or doing special exercises such as swimming 20 circuits of a swimming pool wearing heavy clothing and items of kit. Typical distances to cover each day are around 29km (18 miles), with only hours to complete them, and periods of sleep are ever compressed. The 'highlight' of this period is the 'Long Drag'. The Long Drag takes place on the last day of Route Selection. It begins at midnight, with very little rest from the previous day's march of 15km (9 miles) carrying a 31.7kg (70lb) Bergen. The task ahead of the recruits is to march 64km (40 miles) over the Brecon Beacons in the middle of winter with 24.9kg (55lb) of pack and to complete the distance in 20 hours. As with all the marches of the past weeks, the soldier must also

Adaptive thinking 2

The soldier again faces the need for adaptive thinking, but the configuration of the barbed wire requires another approach using the same tools.

Assault mentality

Although clear thinking is essential for any assault, soldiers must also be able to summon a genuine aggression which has little pity for the enemy. The soldier must also be motivated by an overwhelming desire to see the given objectives achieved.

demonstrate first-class navigational skills using his map and compass, and prove that he can survive in truly inhospitable wilderness.

During this last stage of Route Selection, the trainers will meet the soldier at several points in the journey. At these stages, the trainers are looking for someone who is alert and confident, and someone who knows exactly where he is on the map. This is the quality known in military circles as being 'switched on', and signifies a state of mind that stays alert, focused and motivated despite the body being exhausted. If the candidate can survive the Long Drag physically and mentally, then he will be able to pass through to the 14-week Continuation

Rapid reactions

The rapid-reaction firing range tests the soldier's weapons handling, as well as seeing whether he can distinguish between targets, rather than just randomly firing.

Training in which he will learn the fundamental combat and operational skills of the SAS. This means that he still has a long way to go before the SAS beret can be worn, but the initiation is over and the soldier has demonstrated that he has grit and determination.

The Long Drag is typical of elite forces training, which tends to build up to a single defining moment of endurance and mental testing. Towards the end of a US Marine recruit's period at boot camp, he will have to undergo a final day-long march which takes him to the very brink of exhaustion – recruits in San Diego do a 16km (10 mile) run which includes a steeply inclined section known as the 'Grim Reaper'. US Navy SEALs experience the torments of 'Hell Week', an extraordinarily tough seven-day period of almost no sleep and constant immersion in freezing waters. One special test during this period is 'drown-proofing'. The recruit is thrown into a large, deep swimming pool with his ankles and wrists tied together. In this situation, he must first dive to the bottom of the pool and come back up again for five minutes. He then has to stay afloat for 20 minutes; do underwater back flips for five minutes; retrieve a face mask from the bottom of the pool using his teeth; and finally execute a quick 99m (100yd) swim. In South Africa, the South African Reconnaissance Commandos are left for two nights in the African bush with just a rifle and ammunition, and have to protect themselves from heat exhaustion and wild animals.

The purpose of these tortuous physical exercises is not only to weed out unsuitable candidates, but also to mark out those who are capable of summoning great mental strength when forces are arraigned against them. During SEALs training, recruits are at one point simply left standing in freezing sea water. As their body temperature drops, it is not uncommon for the instructor to make jokes and get all the recruits laughing, only then informing them that laughing increases the outflow of body heat. This treatment may seem exceptionally cruel, but the instructors need to know that the recruit's mind is durable enough to take all manner of knocks and still keep going.

BECOMING THE ELITE

If the recruit passes the initial physical cauldron of basic training, it is at this point that

Training for endurance

Mud-walking is an exhausting exercise used by many armies
to see how long the soldier can maintain his force of will
and keep mounting frustration under control.

he will usually go on to learn the skills that will set him apart from other soldiers. The first phase of training will have demonstrated that the candidate has the toughness essential to endurance operations; the second phase will see if he has the mental acumen to perform some of the most complex military procedures in existence.

Much investment has been made into researching what type of military training gives the soldier the best form of mental preparation for combat. The conclusions have slowly emerged over the past 50 years, but can ultimately be boiled down to two main principles: motivation and realism.

Motivation is vital to military performance. Although the early phases of training tend to attack the recruit's ego and try to get him to fail, during the later skills training, soldiers tend to receive more encourage-

ment and help towards success. Research conducted in the United States and within European armies has emphatically proved that the greatest impetus to perform well during training is to receive the approbation of senior officers and one's peers, as well as access to more benefits such as extra pay or leave. Constant criticism tends to depress any person's level of motivation, so although training remains hard and critical, if the soldier does something right, the trainer will let him know. Praise has the valuable function of giving the soldier confidence and, with confidence, there is an increased self-belief which will be carried forwards into combat.

Perhaps the most vital ingredient to military training is its level of correspondence to the actual conditions of combat. There are two elements to developing realistic combat training that will support a soldier's mental performance in battle. The first of these is that the soldier should have the opportunity to experience as many of the munitions, stresses, decisions and scenarios as he will in a real firefight. This enables the soldier to enter battle without being overwhelmed by unfamiliar noises and sensations. The second is that the training exercises must be repeated again and again until the soldier is performing them without conscious thought. This is what soldiers mean when they speak after battle and say that their 'training took over'. Actions that are repeated constantly become second nature and, even if the soldier is consciously confused, his body will tend to follow familiar actions. The upshot of this is that, in action, the soldier's reflexes become lightning fast, as his subconscious mind tells him what to do well before he has consciously arranged his thoughts.

So, what are the practical methods of instilling the combat mentality in an elite soldier? Central to any elite programme of instruction is that training must both introduce a genuine element of danger and impose pressure upon the soldiers. Live firing exercises are therefore imperative. The Soviet Spetsnaz soldiers were particularly renowned for the brutality of their combat training. During exercises, the Spetsnaz trooper would not only have high-velocity rounds fired close past his head, but explosives and even chemical weapons would be detonated within his vicinity as well. The Spetsnaz training may have taken realism too far – fatalities during instruction were far higher than in most elite units – yet, by the time the soldier qualified for operations, he would to a certain extent know what it is like to have faced death. Such mental hardening would have been tested in campaigns like those which occurred in Afghanistan in the 1980s. More than 4000 Spetsnaz soldiers operated in Afghanistan, conducting raids against mujaheddin rebels holed up in the Afghan mountains. If captured, the Spetsnaz soldiers would face a gruesome and prolonged death at the hands of the

Laser-weapon training

Using laser-firing attachments on firearms enables soldiers to practise shooting at live targets, acclimatising them to putting a human being in their sights and pulling the trigger.

guerrillas, so an incredible level of nerve was required, which in part was derived from training. Similar effects are achieved in the SAS 'killing house' – the training building designed for urban combat and hostage-taking exercises. New officers used to undergo a violent initiation in which they were stood against a wall and told not to move, before an SAS team would burst into the room at speed and empty their H&K MP5s into the wall inches from the junior officer's head. After a fatality, this rite was stopped. Yet, in the killing house's more regular activities, mock assaults are conducted using live ammunition, tear gas and the disorientating G60 stun grenade (this produces an incredible blast of noise and light, and is used as a tactical device to overwhelm terrorists in hostage-taking situations without hurting hostages). These repeated assaults enable the soldiers to become mentally adjusted to the sensations of combat.

Elite soldiers must not only gain experience of being on the receiving end of fire; they must also become accustomed to delivering it. Range marksmanship is all well and good for competition shooting, but soldiers need to accustom themselves to using their weapons in rapid, confusing situations with limited time for either aiming or standard usage. The most typical exercise involves pop-up wooden targets which spring out at the soldier. The trainers will watch to see whether the soldier's reaction time is sharp and also whether he takes in target information before he fires – some of the targets will be civilian forms and there can be harsh penalties for shooting these.

New Technology

Technology, however, has taken fire training to a new level of dynamism. Laser firing systems can now be fitted to the muzzles of assault rifles and each soldier wears a laser receiver in his helmet. When the soldier fires his weapon, loaded with blanks, at his live enemy, the laser also fires. If the target is hit,

the receiver picks up the laser signal, the victim's identity is forwarded to a central computer and his own laser beam is cut off to signal a loss of ammunition and therefore a 'death'. This training device has proved invaluable in most of the world's developed armies. Not only does it enable the soldier to experience the fluidity of combat against a human opponent, but it also lets him actually place a human being in his sights and pull the trigger. Soldiers who perform such training sessions regularly develop much faster reaction skills and the ability to deal with the human factors of warfare.

Psychological training in firearms usage has yielded some interesting results. For instance, at ranges over 50m (164ft), semi-automatic fire produces more kills than automatic fire. Other revelations included the fact that, at night, the three-round burst seems to be the most effective configuration of fire at all ranges. A piece of white tape along the barrel improves night aiming, while men only trained in using tracers in night firing will shoot considerably worse without tracers than those men who have never received tracer training. Ingenious tests have also been devised to test firing abilities under stress. At HumRRO in the United States, an exercise was set up in which a soldier had to hit three bull's-eyes on a target to stop a sequence of dynamite explosions travelling closer and closer towards him. As expected, the closer the blasts came, the more the stress of the approaching blasts impaired the soldier's marksmanship. Elite training aims to overcome this tendency by acclimatising the soldier to the presence of explosions and bullets being discharged so that they no longer disrupt his mental balance. Thus he has an invaluable mental edge when he goes into combat against less-prepared individuals. By being more accustomed to noise and violence, he is therefore less impressed by it and more able to keep a perspective on the

Dark-room combat testing

A unusual test in the 1960s: US soldiers in a darkened room had to respond quickly to 'attacks' from dummies looming out of the darkness. The low light increased the levels of stress involved.

action and make the rapid tactical decisions for which the elite forces are renowned.

TOTAL SKILLS

Training to be an elite soldier means acquiring an enormous breadth and range of skills. Special forces troops require a high degree of intelligence, not just to make tactical pre-

dictions and actions on the spot, but also to apply the sheer diversity of their knowledge. The acquisition of any new skill goes through several phases. First, there is the stage of introduction. Here, the soldier encounters a new skill for the first time and must consciously learn its techniques. Second comes practice. Practising a skill over and over again reinforces the fluency with which the action can be performed. Finally, there is familiarity. At this stage, the practice pays off and the soldier can perform the skill almost without conscious thought: the physical and mental actions have become so familiar that they can be accomplished instinctively.

All elite soldiers must take every skill they are taught to that final stage of familiarity, an enormous task considering the amazing range of techniques and knowledge they must acquire. For example, a typical list of skills for an SAS soldier would include:

- **Weapons expertise.** Just the basic range of weapons which an SAS soldier must know how to strip, maintain and operate includes: M16 assault rifle; M203 grenade launcher; SA80 assault rifle; H&K MP5 submachine-gun; AKM assault rifle; SIG Sauer P226 and Browning Hi-Power pistols; the RPG7 rocket-propelled grenade and LAW rocket; FN MAG and FN Minimi machine-guns; conventional grenades and stun grenades; various sniper rifles; Arwen smoke- and gas-grenade launchers; and demolitions explosives.
- **Communications.** These are communications using radio- and satellite-based means, plus techniques of coding messages, deciphering coded messages and improvising communications in survival situations. Communications also includes how to direct air and artillery strikes.
- **Escape, evasion and survival.** Covered more deeply in Chapter Eight, these three skills involve knowing the means of staying alive in all the world's climates and environments – arctic, temperate, tropical, desert, sea – how to evade the tracking efforts of the enemy and how to resist interrogation if caught.
- **Combat first aid.** As almost all special forces operations are carried out a long way from easy medical evacuation, the soldier has to be conversant with all likely first-aid situations. This can cover everything from treating gunshot wounds and tropical disease to making natural remedies from plants and performing amputations.
- **Reconnaissance and surveillance.** As well as requiring the quality of patience, reconnaissance duties necessitate the knowledge of how to construct observation posts invisible to the enemy, how to identify the military hardware and installations correctly, and then how to decide on the most appropriate course of action in sympathy with the mission. This section of the soldier's skills also includes tracking techniques

The list here refers to only the most fundamental areas of skills; these are added to depending on the type of unit. For example, members of Brazil's 1st Special Forces Counter-Terrorist detachment learn evasive and defensive driving techniques and spend time with Amazonian tribes to hone their jungle survival skills. Austria's GEK, Britain's Special Boat Service (SBS) and Greece's MYK are specially trained in ship boardings (during the Gulf War, MYK troops boarded some 217 freighters in the Red Sea, Persian Gulf and Indian Ocean as part of the enforcement of the UN's import embargo on Iraq). Yet, whatever the type of skill possessed, the soldier must show that he is not a slave to the learning, that he can adapt his skills with flexibility and tenacity when needed.

Ultimately, what instructors look for in elite soldiers is someone who is capable of free-thinking action, reinforced by undoubted combat skills. The time and the money invested in training a special forces soldier is exceptional. The return, however, is someone who has the confidence to accept missions that border on the impossible and execute them with unusual bravery, vigour and confidence.

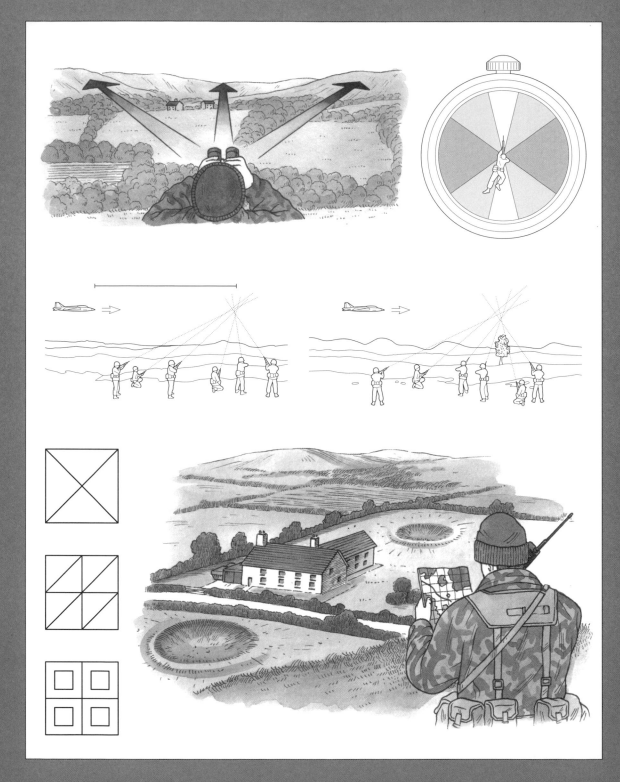

CHAPTER FOUR

Intelligence and Concentration

During World War II, military technology was proved to be one of the deciding factors in battle, culminating in the ultimate low-risk maximum-damage atomic bomb missions that destroyed Hiroshima and Nagasaki in 1945. Since then, weapon systems have continued to develop into demanding tools that require a number of skills to operate successfully.

After 1945, military technologists saw that huge investment in advanced weaponry – both conventional and nuclear – was a way forward in battlefield domination. Consequently, the tools of war rapidly became bigger, faster, more destructive. A Saratoga-class aircraft carrier which had weighed 30,000 tonnes in World War II had, by the 1950s, grown to 60,000 tonnes. World War II tank engines produced 350hp of power; today's equivalents are capable of

1500hp. Advanced munitions such as cluster bombs can now do the equivalent damage in a single aircraft pass to that of a whole flight of World War II fighter-bombers in the 1940s.

The list of technological improvements could go on and on. There is one crucial point here for our study of the military mind. Following World War II, the tools of war became increasingly complex to use and also there were simply more of them. An infantry-man in, say, the Pacific campaign of 1944 would be trained to use his personal weapon (M1 Garand, Thompson M1A1, BAR or M30), basic explosive devices such as grenades, and some other tactical weapons such as the bazooka and the flame-thrower. Today's soldier, by contrast, will have a personal weapon (such as the M16A2, to take a US example), but he or she will also need to be able to use ground-to-air shoulder-launched rockets, guided anti-armour missiles, laser-targeting systems for guiding air-ordnance delivery and very sophisticated computer networks in tactical roles.

The intelligence required to handle these weapons is ever expanding, especially as many of the weapons systems require solid mathematical or computer skills. Nowhere is this truer than within the ranks of elite units. Special forces, because of the nature of their missions and the fact that they tend to attract a higher proportion of the military budget than other personnel, are expected to handle, deploy and understand the most complex weapons on the military market. Yet they must also be able to survive those weapons when used against them. For example, even before they reach their objective, an elite force making an incursion against an enemy coastline must use all their intelligence to negotiate surveillance technologies of incredible sophistication. Over-the-horizon (OTH) radar bounces off the ionosphere to scan the

Sniper's range card

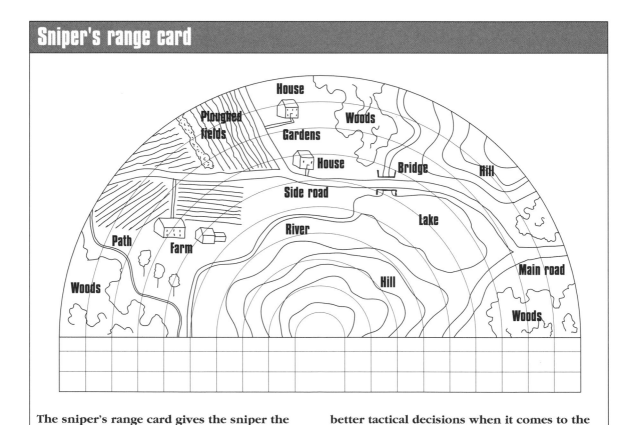

The sniper's range card gives the sniper the ability to 'map' the world in front of him in a clear way. This method serves to support better tactical decisions when it comes to the problems of firing, as well as the challenges of escape and evasion.

airspace up to 6437km (4000 miles) away. Ship- and submarine-borne radar may be guarding against under-water intrusion. AWACS (air-borne warning and control system) aircraft such as the Tu-126 Moss scan the ground and airspace up to a range of 482km (300 miles). An elite insertion team must use incredible tactical and mathematical judgement to work out how to penetrate these defences effectively without being discovered and compromised.

Following the increasing complexity of military weapons systems are a whole other range of diffi-culties which the elite sol-dier must negotiate. The advances in weaponry have led to more demanding tac-tics, where outmanoeuvring an advanced enemy becomes as much a battle of technical acumen as courage. Many elite operations will also be conducted in polit-ically sensitive low-intensity wars where the enemy may well be mixed into the civil-ian population. In such situations, a single misplaced demolitions device can send diplomatic ripples around the world, so the special forces have the additional pressure of mixing military with political objectives. This has been especially true following the Vietnam War, when Vietnamese civilian casualties led to the collapse of domestic and international support for the US effort. Finally, both the speed and distances involved in fighting wars have accelerated and increased, respectively, since World War II. Battlefield data is now more readily avail-able from sophisticated surveillance and

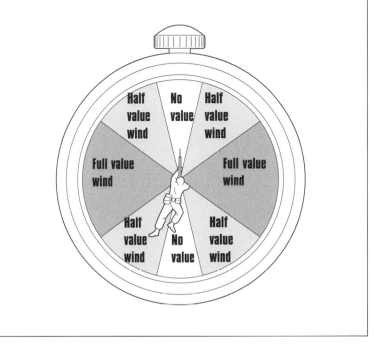

Wind-direction clock system

A sniper makes several complex calculations before he can be confident of a long-distance shot, including wind direction and speed. He can evaluate windage with the clock system.

Half value wind

No value

Half value wind

Full value wind

Full value wind

Half value wind

No value

Half value wind

satellites. The pace of decision-making for soldiers on the ground is relentless and intel-lectually challenging.

This chapter is about the above-average intelligence required to be a modern soldier in an elite regiment. Physical stamina and courage are prerequisites of a special forces operative. Yet without a keen mind, practi-cally trained, the physical and moral efforts will be undone by poor judgement and inef-ficient thought-processes.

TESTING FOR INTELLIGENCE

The professionalisation of military forces since World War II and the related fall in man-power has meant, in many nations, that army, navy and air force recruiters can be much more selective in the personnel they take on board. Academic standards have become much more of a feature in selection processes, although, as we shall see, these are far from the main measure of intelligence. After all, most of the senior-ranking British officers of World War I were the beneficiaries of a public school and university education, but history now dwells upon their appalling tactical ineptitude which sent hundreds of thousands of young men to unnecessary deaths. Surprisingly, well into World War II, there was often an anti-intellectual attitude towards those units which professed themselves specialists. The Special Operations Executive (SOE), Britain's adaptable and courageous secret agent network, spent much of the war trying to convince mainstream military officers to support important and valuable operations. The intolerance for special operations and the secretive skills of its practitioners led to some labelling SOE as 'assassins', while people like Arthur 'Bomber' Harris (Commander in Chief of RAF Bomber Command, 1942–45) resisted using single bombers to aid SOE missions. The root cause of much of this resentment was mistrust for advanced intelligence, which so often seemed to threaten classic military tactics. Since the war, military leaders' decisions have become much more transparent to the world's media, so soldiers have to be seen to be acting intelligently. Also, as we have seen, studies have indicated that more intelligent individuals actually make better fighters in combat. Thus intelligence is now held to be a primary value in elite soldiers.

Most military units have minimum academic standards for entry. US Marines need to score 30-plus on the standard Armed Services Vocational Aptitude Battery (ASVAB) intelligence test, although as 90 per cent of US Marines are high school graduates, two-thirds of entrants have scores of 50-plus. The Royal Marines in the UK usually require officers to have two A levels (equivalent to a US high school diploma) and, commonly, a good honours degree. Opportunities are also usually available for pursuing education once inside the military. In the US Army, for example, most soldiers can access Army Continuing Education System (ACES) courses to study everything from literature and languages to computing and engineering, while pursuing their standard soldiering.

Yet while academic qualifications may indicate the ability to handle difficult concepts, military recruiters will usually be aware that the most adaptable intelligence may not be indicated by school or university performance. Proficiency in subjects such as mathematics and English is usually required to be a soldier, but education cannot indicate some of the other aspects of intelligence which are equally important – perhaps more important – in a good combat soldier:

- **Independent thinker**. Elite soldiers need to show absolute self-reliance and demonstrate that they can think for themselves even if their conclusions seem to fly in the face of conventional wisdom.
- **Creative thinking.** Combat is largely chaos. Soldiers that look beyond obvious solutions to tactical problems (of which the enemy is probably aware) can often control the chaos through creative and innovative thinking. General Gray of the US Marines, author of the influential *Warfighting* manual, states that war is both an art and a science, and the soldier must be able to think in both spheres if he is to be effective.
- **Able to concentrate.** Studies have shown that some very intelligent people show a marked lack of ability to focus on one project for a long time – their minds flit about through boredom and the need for stimulus. Such people would generally make poor elite soldiers, as special forces units require individuals who can lock their concentration onto

one objective and follow it through with total commitment.

- **Able to control emotions.** Although 'emotional intelligence' has become a buzzword in popular psychology, the same quality is required for elite soldiers. Unless the soldier has an essential maturity and the ability to control his own emotions, it is doubtful whether he will be able to give the consistent operational performance required by an elite unit.
- **Strength of mind.** Being able to think effectively is only part of a soldier's

fighting capacity. More important is the nature of those thoughts. If a soldier constantly sees only the odds against him, he is likely to become demotivated and indecisive. If, however, his tenor of thinking is founded on the belief that he can take on any situation and dominate it utterly, he is more likely to succeed with his plans.

These qualities are just some of the elements of intelligence which recruiters look for in military personnel. The selection

Zones of fire range card

This shows a typical range card used by an artillery officer. Handling artillery fire requires a detached sense of control which is not swayed by the power of the detonations. Using the zone card helps develop such an attitude, as well as assisting accurate fire.

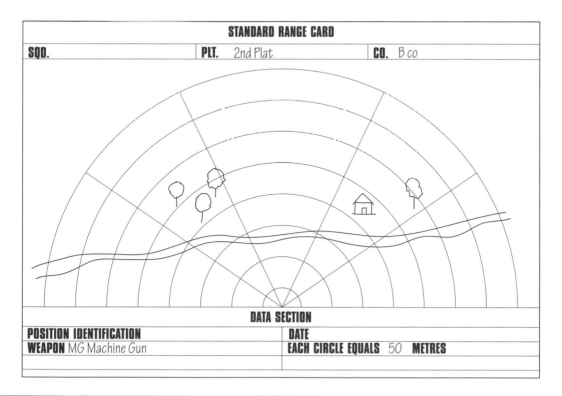

Ground-to-air fire

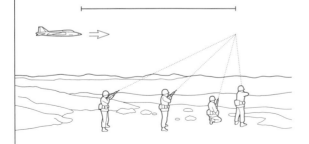

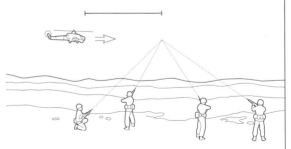

When shooting at helicopters or jets, a group of soldiers must be able to determine a point in time and space through which the aircraft

must fly. With jets, that point is about 200m (219yds) from the nose; with helicopters it is a distance of about 50m (55yds).

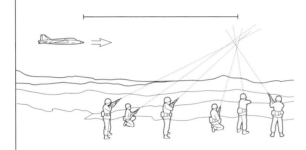

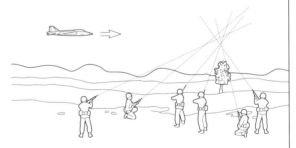

The small-arms fire aimed from the ground can be co-ordinated by using a visual reference point on the landscape as a line of

fire. In the case illustrated here, the soldiers are using a tree as a marker, gathering a storm of bullets above it.

process for soldiers (especially elite soldiers) tends to examine both practical and abstract intelligence. Abstract intelligence – powers of reasoning, logic and deduction – can be tested through standard IQ tests. A range of these is used throughout the world and their contents are usually classified. However, they are known to consist of a straightforward run of tests and the results are a good indicator of

the applicant's linguistic, mathematical, logical and observational skills. Yet paper tests are only one method of reaching an assessment.

In the Royal Marines, all officer candidates are subjected to the three-day Admiralty Interview Board (AIB) aboard HMS *Sultan* in Gosport, Hampshire. The board consists of a panel of highly critical (and unsmiling) RM officers, plus a psychologist, a civilian headmaster and an RM careers officer. Over three days, the candidate is put through an exhausting sequence of verbal interviews, mental tests and assessments of his general knowledge and his knowledge of RM history. Weakness in any area will be ruthlessly exploited and evaluated, mainly to see how the candidate's intelligence stands up to being placed under extremes of pressure. A typical exercise would include being asked how a group of survivors on a desert island might live through their ordeal and be rescued. Every twist and turn in the candidate's logic is queried and analysed by the board until the candidate twists himself into logical knots. That his logic is shaky is not necessarily a problem; how he handles himself emotionally in argument is what is important.

All candidates for elite forces have their practical intelligence and their theoretical intelligence tested. There is little difference between the two, for practical intelligence is generally a test of whether theoretical intelligence is actually working. The elements which make up practical training are explored more fully in the previous chapter. To summarise, recruits for the special forces are trained by simulating actual battlefield circumstances, with real stress and real danger being constantly present. In all special forces, mock battles of varying scales and sizes are played out to see whether the soldier's thought-processes stay clear under fire. In the US Marine Corps boot camp, groups of soldiers fight against one another in mock battles, realism provided by 0.11kg (0.25lb) blocks of explosive being detonated around them and live ammunition being fired over their heads. All the while, instructors observe the soldiers' ability to handle pressurised decision-making environments.

Defensive thinking

The diagram here shows an all-round defence procedure for use when disembarking from a helicopter. Combat intelligence often consists of predicting worst possible outcomes and adapting tactics to this prediction.

Through this mix of practical and theoretical testing, recruiters gain a good overall picture of the levels of intelligence and concentration which an individual will be able to muster in battle. But let us return to specifics. What are the individual intelligence skills that a soldier must possess to make him a part of the elite? Basically, an elite soldier must possess the following qualities of mind if he is to make it as a special forces operative:

- mathematical intelligence
- communication skills
- technical intelligence
- tactical intelligence
- focus

Now we will turn our attention to why each of these individual types of thinking or attitude is required on the modern battlefield. Once we have assessed each type of intelligence, then we will look at how all of them come together in one particular mode of special forces operation: sniping.

Mathematical Intelligence

The modern soldier almost invariably cannot escape the need to use mathematical skills. Even the act of navigation alone – a basic requirement for any soldier on land, sea or air – needs someone to calculate angles, distance and time. The list of activities for the elite soldier which require good mathematical intelligence is extensive and includes:

- navigation
- estimating logistical requirements
- artillery/airstrike control
- coding messages
- range finding
- estimating enemy troop strength during surveillance

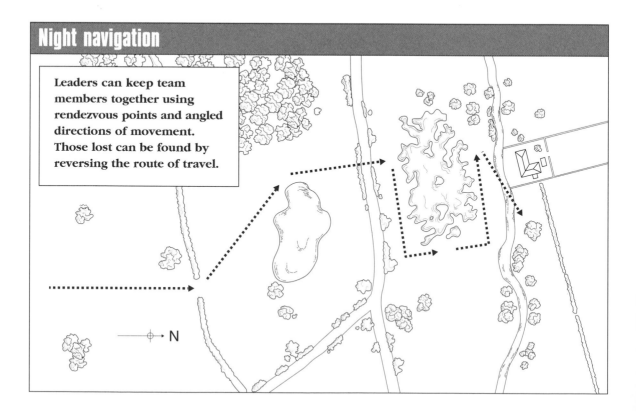

Night navigation

Leaders can keep team members together using rendezvous points and angled directions of movement. Those lost can be found by reversing the route of travel.

N

Visual intelligence

When viewing terrain through binoculars, the ground is scanned from right to left, increasing towards the horizon. Key features are memorised and reported.

This list is not exhaustive. It will be noticed that mathematical skills are as essential to actual combat performance as they are to barrack-based duties. Good illustrations of this are the activities of directing anti-aircraft fire using small arms and artillery control.

Shooting down modern jets using only personal weapons or machine guns is diffi-cult in the extreme. A modern strike fighter can be moving at the speed of sound when it draws past in the attack, so to hit it from a standing position using only an assault rifle is fairly implausible. Yet it can be done, and elite soldiers are trained in aircraft-downing techniques which use processes of mathe-matical judgement. The speed of the aircraft

Mapping the terrain

Tactical decisions are made more simple by mapping the crucial environmental and tactical features. This cuts out surplus data and allows the clear sight of objectives.

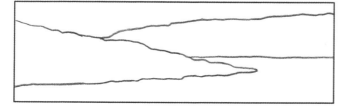

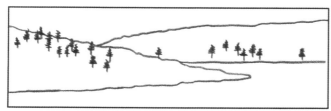

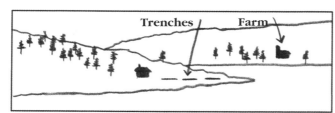

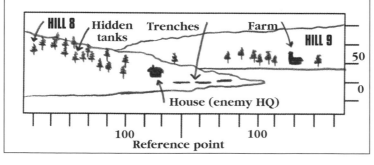

Reference point

the ground. Thus, against jets, soldiers need to calculate a point approximately 200m (656ft) from the front of the aircraft at a particular moment of its flight, and then concentrate a shower of small arms rounds into that point so that the aircraft then flies through the hail.

To calculate that distance, the soldier can either do a visual multiplication of the length of the aircraft (which should ideally be known by the special forces soldier) or use techniques such as placing the index finger over the centre of the image of the flying aircraft (for a standard fighter, if only the nose and tail overlap the finger, the aircraft is about 350m (1148ft) away).

This example is a matter of basic distance calculation using techniques of visual estimation, rather than a distinct mathematical process. More advanced mathematical techniques are applied in field tactics, especially when the soldier needs to define his position in relation to a particular target (say, for the purposes of artillery control). If the soldier needs to calculate how far he is from a target object, he first takes a compass reading on the target. Then he moves parallel to the target until the compass reading to the target changes in either direction by 45 degrees. Using basic geometry, the soldier can now work out that the distance between the point of his original reading

cuts out the possibility of directly aiming at the aircraft; by the time the bullets get to the point of aim, the jet has already passed that point. What is needed is for the aircraft to fly into the stream of bullets coming up from

Controlling artillery

This requires mathematics, ballistics, communications and munitions skills. The controller must 'walk-in' the fire onto the target by giving instructions on range and bearing to the firebase.

and the point of his 45-degree angle reading is actually the same distance as that from his starting point to his target.

Similar techniques can be used to estimate the height of target features such as buildings and aerial masts. Once the distance between observer and object is known, the soldier holds up a pencil at arm's length and marks the visual height on the pencil. This height is then measured in centimetres. The distance between the pencil in the hand and the observer's eye is also measured. These two measurements actually form an angle between eye and pencil proportionately equal to the angle between observer and the top of the target. Again, turning to geometry, 'a' equals the height measured on the pencil, 'b' equals the distance between pencil and eye, 'A' equals the height of the target and 'B' equals the distance to the target. Thus the equation a/b x B = A will yield a good estimation of the target height.

These two examples show how acts of mathematical intelligence are written into the fighting ability of an elite soldier. Thus, numeracy is thoroughly tested before any individual can become a member of a special forces unit.

Angles in artillery control

A soldier can utilise his fingers to measure angles for artillery control if there are no technical aids. There are 6400 mils (a unit of measurement) in a circle, and one mil is an angular distance of one metre at 1000m. The diagram shows how the hand can be used to calculate mils and then transfer this into distance.

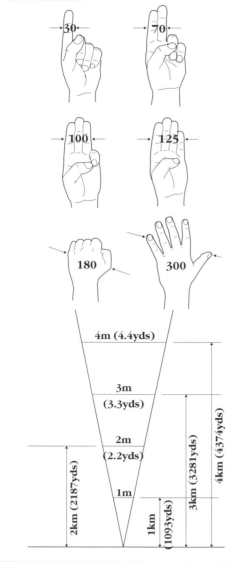

Communication Skills

Communication skills are invaluable in all walks of life, not just soldiering. Most intelligence tests for military units contain some element of linguistic or comprehension assessment. The would-be soldier needs to demonstrate that he has control over language and its meaning. The assessors will be aware that the ability to put together coherent, easily understood sentences and understand complex orders when received means that the soldier will be able to shape tactics with confidence, rather than add to battlefield confusion.

Intelligent use of language for the elite soldier often means that they acquire foreign languages to aid in international missions.

Calculations in range-finding

How to calculate range and height of a target (see main text): mathematical skills are an often forgotten part of the Special Forces portfolio, but they are vital.

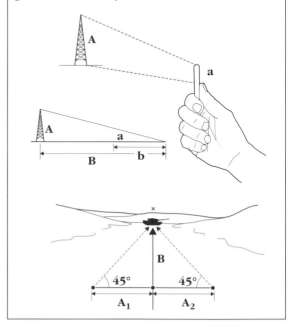

Memory exercise – British Army (1940s)

Observe a shape, one every few seconds. Cover them over. Try to draw as many from memory as possible. This is good training in both observation and recall.

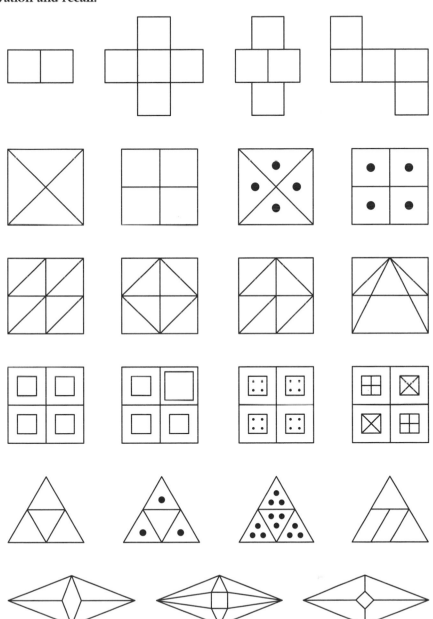

Linguistic test

An example of a language puzzle used by Special Forces recruitment papers. Try to crack the code of this puzzle to reveal a comprehensible sentence.

Vjg iriqc jt up vjg ohiw jpero.

Acquiring another language for military use need not be difficult, as, unless the soldier is working undercover or he is participating in advanced social programmes, then all he needs is a basic working vocabulary and grammar. During the Vietnam War, studies were conducted in the US Army into the minimum Vietnamese-language requirements for soldiers to be able to conduct basic interrogation and liaison. Knowledge of 450 words was found to be sufficient in most cases to sustain a basic conversation.

In terms of practical languages, English, French and Spanish are the most useful trio. These languages linger in the extensive former colonies of the three countries and English itself has been adopted as the international language of business and commerce. Many SAS soldiers attend the British Army School of Languages to acquire different languages suited to their operational destinations. Arabic, Malay and Norwegian are three of the most popular languages, and vocabulary of between 500 and 1000 words of each plus a knowledge of the essential grammar enable the soldiers to converse with some degree of confidence and versatility.

Technical Intelligence

The issue of technical intelligence in many ways links us back to our opening points concerning the advances in weapons technology. The simplest assault rifle may consist of hundreds of parts, including many delicate mechanisms such as gas-operation systems and cartridge extractors. Being able to maintain and use this weapon is the thin end of the technical wedge for the elite soldier. Special forces troops are called on to perform duties which encompass the roles of several soldiers in the regular army. Thus, while a regular army unit may have a field medic, driver and demolitions expert as separate individuals, in the special forces, these roles will often be performed by the same man. Furthermore, elite soldiers may have to engage in unusual technical pursuits as part of their operational portfolio. Members of the US Army's secretive Delta Force, for example, are not only obliged to understand the technicalities of modern weapons, but also have to pick up several specialist skills which rely on good manual dexterity and the ability to understand engineering principles. Examples include lockpicking – a skill essential for silent entry assault operations – and other more dramatic talents such as how to drive racing cars and even trains. Because Delta soldiers are also on hand for aircraft hostage situations, they are trained in how to supply an aircraft with aviation fuel and hydraulic

Number test – British Army (1940s)

Fill in the blanks in these sequences of numbers. Such tests are commonly used to evaluate general intelligence and numeracy amongst army recruits.	3	5	6	10	9	15	…	…
	1	2	6	12	36	72	…	…
	1	4	10	22	46	94	…	…
	1	2	6	21	88	445	…	…
	4	7	15	31	63	127	…	…

fluid. When it comes to building assaults, they must know how to ascend or descend the face of the tallest skyscrapers.

The Delta Force example shows why the elite soldier needs to possess practical knowledge and a capacity to turn the mind to handling what are essentially engineering problems at any moment during an operation. Even skills such as demolitions – involving the actual destruction of buildings, bridges etc. – need to be based on comprehension of factors such as structural loading, points of tension and material properties in order to be conducted successfully.

Tactical Intelligence

Tactical intelligence is covered more fully in later chapters, but suffice to say that it is one of those aspects of military intelligence which is taught, rather than natural. Yet there are ingredients of being a good tactician that come from personality, rather than learning. One of the key ingredients is being able to make decisions. Most elite training programmes place the recruits into pressurised decision-making environments from the moment they step off the bus. At US Marine Corps boot camp, for instance, a recruit may well find himself between two instructors who are shouting apparently contradictory and impossible commands at him. The purpose is not just to see if the recruit will break under the pressure, but also to see if he can make a decision and then stick to it. The Marines are taught the 'rule of three' when making decisions – come up with three possible solutions to every problem (no more, no less), look at the pros and cons of each, then choose one and stick with it. This technique has extraordinary success and, by the time the recruits become Marines, they are very comfortable with handling decision-making at every level.

Tactical intelligence is a massive subject and requires everything from a good eye for detail, a strong memory and the ability to visualise problems and solutions to a capacity to organise and also the tendency to be able to stick with one's choice. However, it is a common misperception that tactics should be complex and overtly daring. The acronym 'KISS' is prevalent in the US forces, standing for 'Keep it simple, Stupid'. The penalties of overcomplex tactical efforts can be seen at their most tragic in Delta Force's Operation Eagle Claw in 1980. American hostages were being held in the US Embassy in Tehran, Iran. Delta Force was charged with their rescue and produced a plan consisting of several stages. First, the soldiers were to be flown in a flight of seven MC-130E transport aircraft (three for Delta, three for fuel and one carrying

Calculating aircraft distance

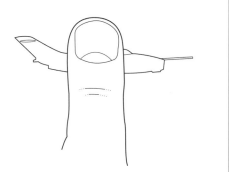

A fighter aircraft's distance can be judged using the forefinger. With a MiG 21, if the finger covers from the start of the tailplane to the cockpit's front, it is 350m (1148ft) away.

a company of US Rangers) from Masirah Island off the coast of Oman to a base (Desert 1) about 320km (200 miles) from Tehran. Once there, eight RH-53D helicopters from USS *Nimitz* would arrive, refuel, then transport them to a secret location just outside Tehran where they would wait to effect a night attack against the enemy. During this time, the Rangers would have secured Manzariyeh airfield 48km (30 miles) south of Tehran. It was intended that, after the rescue of the hostages, the helicopters would airlift the soldiers and freed embassy officials to Manzariyeh, where a C-141 Starlifter transporter would fly everyone out.

The complexity of the plan made it open to many problems, although much of what subsequently happened was down to bad luck as much as bad judgement. Arrival at Desert 1 on 24 April found not an unused strip of desert road, but an active route. A passenger bus with 30 Iranian civilians had to be captured and held. A Ranger ended up firing an LAW anti-tank rocket into an fleeing petrol tanker, although the driver actually escaped in a smaller truck. Compounding

this loss of surprise, only six of the helicopters arrived, half an hour late. One of these then had mechanical problems and one, tragically, collided with a MC-130E; eight US servicemen died in the resulting blast. The mission was then called off and the hostages in the US embassy were later released after negotiations.

Eagle Claw was blighted by unfortunate accidents, but military observers have since commented that the mission was too complicated, relying on too many sequences of complex events to be successful. The lesson was a hard one, but elite missions today try to strip tactics down to the bare minimum, relying instead on tempo and hard-hitting combat skills. Those who are members of elite regiments need to show that they can think in clear tactical movements and develop plans that are workable from insertion to escape.

Focus and Concentration

Concentration is needed by all soldiers, but none more so than those belonging to elite units. Elite operations have a surgical quality to them, and frequently require the soldiers to operate on their own and face considerable periods of inactivity. Boredom and restlessness thus become genuine enemies to concentration, and only if the soldier can resign himself to these and keep his mind lively and alert will he be effective in his role. All elite soldiers are screened for the ability to concentrate. Particularly revealing exercises into the relationship between personality and concentration were conducted in Northern Ireland from the 1960s to the 1980s to do with the recruitment of bomb disposal personnel. People who were discovered to have feelings of resentment at some past incident in their lives, or those who had a fascination with elements such as fire, wind, or storms, were generally unsuitable for bomb disposal; the psychologists found that, under pressure, the disposal officer's

Using tracer fire

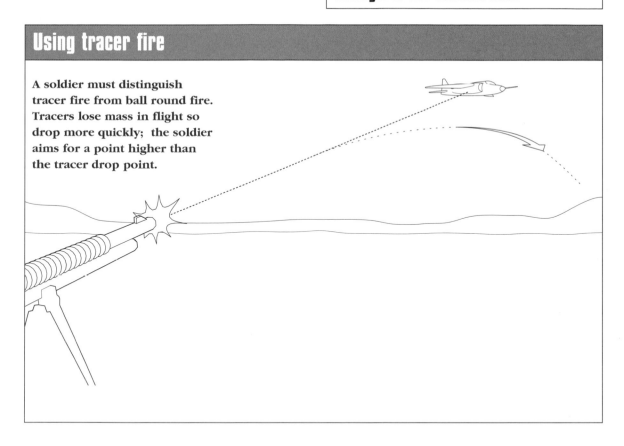

A soldier must distinguish tracer fire from ball round fire. Tracers lose mass in flight so drop more quickly; the soldier aims for a point higher than the tracer drop point.

attention could be pulled away from his task by either suicidal thoughts or a fascination with the potential explosion. These thoughts may well be in the back of the soldier's mind, but even this is enough to distract him. Psychologists also found that successful EOD (explosive ordnance officers) demonstrated an eye for detail, an enjoyment of manual dexterity and the ability to distinguish objects out of place against their background.

Similar principles apply to elite soldiers. To show the concentration needed for special operations, they must be balanced and composed, and able to direct their attention at will to their chosen task. Nonetheless, their minds should also remain flexible and not become fixated on one course of action.

So how do the above forms of intelligence actually come together in an operational role? To see them in action, we shall now turn to one of the most demanding of special forces roles: sniping. As we shall see, sniping requires that all aspects of the elite intelligence unit in one smooth-functioning operation. To see this clearly, we shall run through the list of intelligence qualities above once more, applying them this time specifically to the sniper's role.

SNIPING
Mathematical Skills
Mathematical calculations and deduction feature surprisingly highly in the sniping mission. First, the soldier must accurately calculate the distance between himself and his

target. This he can do using the method above, using map coordinates or, if he is being fired upon, by a simple calculation. When being fired at, the crack of the bullet is heard before the blast of the rifle. The further the shooter is away, the longer the time between the two noises. Working on the basis of a high-velocity (3000fps+) rifle being fired, a sound gap of one second indicates that the shooter is about 630m (2060ft) away. Using this as a landmark, the sniper can calculate other distances and position himself correctly (snipers generally fire at ranges of more than 500m (1640ft) to avoid detection upon firing).

Once he has a target distance, the sniper must calibrate his sights to perform correctly at that distance, and he must also make an allowance for windage. Calculating windage (the influence of wind upon the flight of a bullet) begins with estimating wind speed and direction. This can be done by tying a piece of cloth to a tree or other mast, and then measuring the rough angle the cloth assumes from the tree and dividing this angle by four to get the wind velocity in miles per hour. With this measurement, he can calculate what windage adjustment in minutes (a unit of measurement) to make using the formula: range (R) multiplied by wind speed (V) divided by 15 (for distances up to 457m/1500ft), 14 (550m/1800ft), 13 (640–732m/2100–2400ft), 12 (823m/2700ft) or 11 (914m/3000ft). Once the soldier has made all of these calculations, he is able to confidently deliver an accurate shot.

Communication Skills

Communication skills are perhaps not the most obvious intelligence quality for the solitary profession of sniper, but one which makes more sense within urban counterterrorist and hostage-taking situations. When there are multiple targets, the many snipers employed need to relate their opportunities for fire to each of the other snipers and the communications centre. By doing so, each sniper can fire simultaneously and, in an ideal world, take out all the terrorists in one wave of fire. For example, during a hostage situation in Somalia when guerrillas took 28 French schoolchildren hostage on a bus, French GIGN snipers shot four terrorists in the head simultaneously with 7.62-mm FR-F1 rifles. Such coordination required clear expressions of intent from each sniper and an awareness of his position as part of a team.

Technical Intelligence

A sniper must be an absolute master of his rifle. He must know how it fires, how it is maintained, how the weather might affect its performance, what heat build-up in the barrel will do to its accuracy, and how to get the best out of the sights fitted (including telescopic, optical and thermal imaging sights). His technical awareness must also extend to such factors as the best clothes to wear for the sniping role (soft cloth to stop branches making a noise when rubbing against the material, and tightly fitted at wrists and ankles to avoid snagging), and how to construct a natural hide to best conceal his position.

Sometimes, a sniper will also be used in anti-materiel roles – especially if he is armed with one of the new breed of enormously powerful sniper rifles such as the .50 calibre Barrett M82A1 which can punch through an engine block at distances well in excess of 1.6km (1 mile). In this capacity, the soldier will have to possess enough technical knowledge to identify the most structurally vulnerable point on, for example, a satellite communications system and then be able to put a round into that point at extended distances.

Tactical Intelligence

The two main tactical considerations for a sniper are 1) how to get into position to be able to deliver the shot; and 2) how to get out of the area safely once the shot has been fired. Both considerations must organise the tactical intelligence of the soldier. For example, he must select a position in which he is obscured from view, with a clear line of fire to the target, but also position his gun so that the blast from firing will not raise dust and consequently reveal his whereabouts. Ideally, once the shot is taken, he should be able to fall back over the brow of a hill or disappear into dense woodland.

In a hostage-rescue setting, the tactical priorities shift towards preserving the safety of the hostages. This means assuming a sniping position high up on buildings, the theory being that, with a steep angle of fire, the bullet will pass through the terrorist and quickly bury itself in the floor a short distance from him and not go on to endanger the safety of those held captive. If shooting from behind a car, the sniper will position himself automatically behind the engine block to provide himself with the strongest protection should fire be returned. If shooting from a window, the sniper will not stand directly in the windowsill – where he would be fully visible and framed for a terrorist shot – but stand back in the room where his silhouette will be darkened and less prominent to observers outside the building.

As we can see, the final act of aiming and pulling the trigger is only part of a long tactical process in which the sniper must engage and he must use considerable judgement from the beginning of the operation to give himself the highest chances of surviving a mission.

Focus and concentration

Once the moment does finally arrive for the sniper to aim and take the shot at his intended target, his levels of concentration must be at their optimum. To assist his aiming, the sniper should control his breathing properly. This should be carried out in the following way:

- **1.** Draw in a deep breath and let it out calmly.
- **2.** Draw in another deep breath, but this time hold it for a second, then let it out naturally but slowly.
- **3.** At the bottom of the breath is a natural pause before breathing begins again and the body is very still and calm. In this moment, pull the trigger.

By assisting his concentration with breathing, the soldier should be in a perfect mental and physical state to take his shot. Of course, his concentration will have been exercised before this moment by activities such as targeting and even waiting for the target to appear. Remember, the target may be exercising all the fieldcraft skills of the elite soldier himself, so a sharp eye is required to stop the sniper becoming a victim of a sniping attack himself.

Despite the tension of sniping, boredom is possibly the greatest enemy to the sniper in the effective execution of his role. Once he is bored, concentration lapses and then mistakes can be made. Thus, the genuinely proficient sniper is a rare breed indeed and this role therefore requires men of exceptional mental stamina.

NEED TO BE ADAPTABLE

The example of the sniper is only one of many possible illustrations of mental intelligence in action that we could take from looking at the elite units. The soldiers from special forces necessarily have to be supremely adaptable and psychologically dextrous if they are to stand any chance of survival in the hostile environments which they have to frequent.

It is hard to think of any other 'job' in this world which equals the mental and physical demands of the elite soldier, and therefore they deserve our genuine respect for the very large capabilities that their minds must possess.

CHAPTER FIVE

Building a Team Mind

Teamwork is essential for success, particularly for small special forces teams operating in hostile or potentially hostile environments. On 9 April 1973, elite Israeli soldiers from the exceptional Sayeret Mat'kal special forces unit demonstrated the principles of teamwork in a bloody and ruthlesslessly efficient manner during a counterterrorist operation.

The operation they were involved in was motivated by revenge. The early 1970s were a period of virulent terrorism within Israeli borders and against Israeli-linked targets worldwide, with multiple Islamic, Arabic and Palestinian factions venting their anger against Israeli civilian and military targets. This culminated in the massacre of Israeli athletes at the Munich Olympics, an act which stunned the world and mobilised Israel to mount Operation Spring of Youth.

This was to be one of the largest counter-terrorist operations the world had ever seen, and the first target was those who had masterminded the Munich massacre.

The leaders and members of the Palestinian 'Black September' terrorist organisation were living in an expensive district of West Beirut. Their flats were well protected by bodyguards both inside and out, these men being all too aware that Israel could be contemplating action against their forces.

Sayeret Mat'kal operatives knew that deception and fast, stunning violence was the only way to take out the Black September leaders. Dressed in civilian clothes, they waited outside the Black September apartments in three rented Opel cars, nothing on their person connecting them with Israel; the mission was a political minefield (even their Ingram Mac-10 and AK-47 weapons were traceable only to Palestinian or Syrian sources). When the time came to act, they did so with cunning and co-operation, two of the defining features of special forces operations.

A group of male and female agents, the men dressed like hippies and the women dressed seductively, walked casually up to the PLO guards who were sat in two black Mercedes in front of the apartments. The women had been selected for their physical allure, and the guards engaged in some flirtation. It was the last thing they would ever do.

Seconds later, one of the guards had been shot through the head by a .22 pistol round and two other guards mown down by fire from the agents in the cars. All the gunfire so far had been silenced, but one stray round had penetrated the bonnet of a Mercedes and triggered its horn; their cover was blown.

Sayeret Mat'kal operational planning is exhaustive, so allowances had been made for such a potential disaster. The agents scattered to positions around the streets to guard against reinforcements, while dedicated teams rushed into apartments on opposite sides of the street to find and eliminate their targets. One group of four men, led by Major Yoni Netanyahu, rushed straight to the sixth-floor apartment of creator of the Munich massacre, Abu Yusef, and blew the door off with specially prepared charges. Major Netanyahu machine-gunned Abu Yusef to death in front of his wife and children, while the other men

Team reconnaissance

A good example of team thinking. Each member acts in a supporting role to each other, with the flank men protecting the central advance with 360 degree coverage.

searched out important files and paperwork. Across the street, two other teams were killing Black September frontmen Kamal A'dwan and Kamal Nasser with a similar bloody efficiency. Down in the street, Israeli agents and Lebanese troops were by this time engaged in a ferocious street battle. Yet once the assault teams had completed their work, an incredible display of driving by men from Mossad (the Israeli secret service) took all the agents at speed out of the firefight and down to the Mediterranean coast. There, Israeli special forces frogmen had deposited dinghies which the agents then used to make their escape.

This stunning raid by Sayeret Mat'kal has many military virtues: good intelligence, effective use of weaponry, courage. Yet what stands out most is the impressive level of integration between the team members, even under incredible pressure and violence. If any one element of the attack force had been weak and failed in its objectives – if the guards on the street had not been successfully killed or thc frogmcn had not deposited the dinghies in the right place –the mission would have almost certainly spiralled into disaster.

THE 'TEAM MIND'

Thc co-opcration and unity displayed by the Israeli soldiers in this mission illustrates one of the key factors in what makes an elite team more than just a collection of highly trained individuals. Special forces have to rely on each other implicitly in the field and, if the soldier does not develop the 'team mind', he will deprive the unit of confidence in one another. If this happens, the unit will have a gap in its defences that will render it vulnerable.

The US Navy SEALs have a saying that 'There is no "I" in team or SEAL'. This chapter is about how elite units develop or target that team-centred attitude which puts the welfare of others first and rejects egocentric

File formation

In this formation the line of advancing soldiers must place great trust in the reconnaissance troops on the flanks to warn and protect them from any emergent dangers.

or attention-grabbing mentalities. This is not to say that a competitive nature has no place within elite forces; most elite soldiers strive to be the best of their units. Yet the history of elite operations has shown that, unless a special force units coheres as a team, its likelihood of being a military success and achieving its goals is almost nil.

SMALL IS BEAUTIFUL

As in so many other areas, psychological research into the nature of military units really achieved prominence in the period immediately after World War II. World War II had provided leaders and military thinkers with information about the performance of all manner of units, from two-man behind-the-lines teams to divisional-strength manoeuvres. It had become clear that many different factors fed into an effective combat squad; however, if a group of fighting-focused men truly united in a single grouping, their worth was tenfold that of less motivated units. So what is it that makes a group of different soldiers become a team? And how does the outlook of elite forces' teams differ from that of regular units?

The first thing to note about military units is that, when people are in groups, they behave in radically different ways to when people are on their own. From a military point of view – and studies at West Point in the United States have confirmed this – group behaviour tends to be less restrained than individual behaviour. Military atrocities, for instance, are very rarely committed by unobserved individuals, but usually by groups of people whose emotions start feeding off one another until they find themselves in the grip of violent emotions they had not previously known. In the civilian world, riots have been demonstrated to be caused by the same effect, as explained in a later chapter. The specific problem which was discovered by the various studies was that groups of people tend to become more

emotionally 'wound up' and, once they are aggravated, that emotion will remain for a longer period than if individuals were left to themselves. One US soldier from Vietnam recounts the grim tale of how he shot an old Vietnamese woman tending her crops just because he was dared to do so. Afterwards, he was stunned that he could have performed such a hideous act. The action only made sense amongst the group, a body of people typically having less self-control than people on their own.

In the past, particularly in the 1960s when elite forces were being formed to cope with the extremities of counterinsurgency in Vietnam, such excessive aggression was actively fostered in some units. During World War II, the British Home Guards' manual recommended that killing the enemy by bayonet or club was preferable to shooting them because of the effect on enemy morale produced by the mutilated corpse. Lieutenant William Calley – a participant in the infamous My Lai massacre – told the military court of the US Marine Corps unarmed combat training in which men would be significantly injured by high-power kicks and punches to vital areas. Apocryphal stories from Vietnam tell of training regimes in the special forces where groups of men had to torture and kill harmless domestic animals as a toughening exercise. Even today, legal action was recently taken against some US elite units for gruesome initiation rituals such as pinning badges directly into a soldier's chest.

Perhaps the most famously aggressive unit is the French Foreign Legion. Life for recruits is particularly hard. Some exercises have involved crawling through filth-filled ditches while the seasoned soldiers stand on the side and urinate onto the men below. Beatings from NCOs can be harsh punishments and it is reputed that no soldier who trains in the legion will finish his training without at some point soaking his

Spearhead formation

Holding a pattern such as the spearhead formation shown below requires discipline, as well as the ability to accept responsibility for each position. If one member of the group is weak, then the whole group is consequently vulnerable.

socks with his own blood. The French Foreign Legion is certainly one of the fiercest of the world's elite units, but many military observers have argued that it is at the expense of its military skills. Many legionnaires often feel degraded and abused, and the desertion rate currently runs at one in eight.

SELF-CONTROL

We can straight away see the problem of overly aggressive training for elite units. Elite operations require a maximum of self-control. If the group gets carried away with personal emotions or blind rage, it is likely that vital operational data or objectives will be either overlooked or mishandled. Yet another conclusion of the research was that the more actual combat a group had seen, the more able they were to control their emotions and actions in battle. In this light, the harsh training of elite units makes even more sense. Putting soldiers through tough, realistic and punishing training not only makes the individual men harder, fitter and stronger, but it also makes the group more accustomed to meeting stress and violence as part of their natural behaviour. As the group adjusts to combat, wayward emotions become less acceptable and the soldiers start to achieve a self-control that bonds the group members together. This we saw in the opening illustration of the Israeli operation. The targets of the Sayeret Mat'kal agents were people who had committed appalling atrocities against the Israeli state and people. Yet, during the mission, each soldier did not let the desire for outright revenge cloud their team-mindedness. Although the assassinations were performed brutally, they were performed without any excesses of action or rage.

Much of the research into the psychology of military units was conducted in the Korean War and one particular conclusion that emerged was of special relevance to elite forces teams. Tests were conducted at the front line to find out what size squad was the most conducive to stability, uniformity and fighting spirit. When a group became too large, say, the size of a company (around 120 men), the cohesion was lessened because the unit was too big to develop personal bonds between all the individuals. The conclusion seemed to be that the best form of fighting group consisted of single-figure units, ideally groups of between three and eight men (five was actually decided as the optimum size). Within a smaller group, the attitudes, expectations and combat talents tended to show a greater degree of conformity. This meant that each member tended to pull his weight in equal measure with the others, and this in turn added up to a much more effective combat unit because there were no weak links.

The lesson was a valuable one for elite units, even though it was also a lesson they perhaps already knew. Many special forces units work in operational teams of rarely more than 10, unless on a particularly major operation. These men will have trained together, fought together and experienced the shared grief of lost friends. As such, they

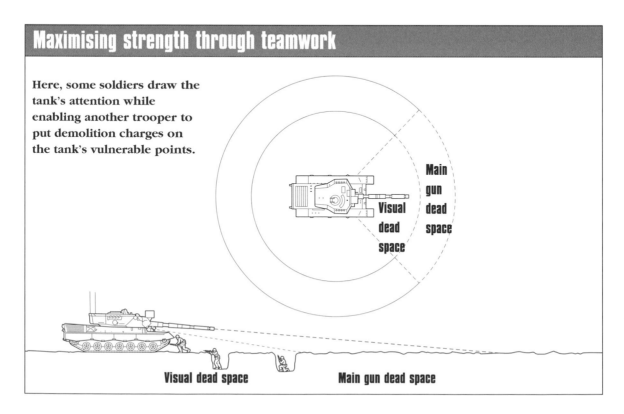

Maximising strength through teamwork

Here, some soldiers draw the tank's attention while enabling another trooper to put demolition charges on the tank's vulnerable points.

Main gun dead space

Visual dead space

Visual dead space

Main gun dead space

tend to show unique levels of trust in one another and also the tactical ability to let others take over a role if they are better qualified to do so. The lesson that 'small is beautiful' seems to have sunk through to even those elite forces which tend to operate on a more regular scale. The US Marine Corps, for instance, is capable of enormous multi-arm manoeuvres, but regardless of the size of force, it is still governed by what it calls the 'rule of three'.

The rule of three means that a Marine leader has basic responsibility for only three individuals or subunits. Thus, a Marine private belongs to a three-person fire team. A Marine corporal has responsibility for that fire team. A sergeant must exercise control over a squad of three fire teams. A staff sergeant or lieutenant leads a platoon made up of three squads. Although the number of people involved expands every time you go further up the ladder of rank, the system means that each person has a limited responsibility to an identifiable group of people. The effect of this is that the US Marines have a very close-knit relationship with one another and a dedication to their immediate network of three. Not only does this breed the esprit de corps for which the US Marines are so famed, but it also helps to make decision-making clear and efficient, which is obviously a vital factor in the performance of a military unit.

Not all elite units operate on similar principles, but generally there are codes of individual responsibility to each other which make real tactical sense once applied in combat. On the smallest scale possible, the SAS operates a 'buddy-buddy' system within all its operations, where two or more people are involved. Especially in arctic warfare or anti-guerrilla operations, the soldiers are teamed up in pairs, with each soldier having responsibility for protecting his partner and also for stepping in if the partner is killed or injured. Although the buddy-buddy system is actually a safeguard for the mission when personnel could be lost in action, it also has the psychological effect of reassurance in knowing that another set of eyes are looking out for you.

A SENSE OF BELONGING

Although there are many ways of organising a military unit to aid its efficiency, not all groups turn into effective combat squads. Sometimes the opposite is the case. We have already noted elsewhere the problem of 'fragging' in US units during the Vietnam War, whereby officers were being deliberately killed in firefights by their own men using fragmentation grenades. Fragging had many causes: low morale, high casualty rates in some units, the inexperience of junior officers, drug abuse and sheer malice. What these incidents taught was that groups did not automatically come together and that antagonisms would seriously impair the performance of the squad in combat.

By contrast, when psychologists in the Korean War set out to define the qualities of those squads who had proved themselves in combat, what they found was that each member had a sense of belonging to his unit and a sense of personal closeness to his comrades. In short, men tend to have to like each other as people before they can become a truly effective combat squad. The relationship between each man is not always the same. For instance, one person may be valued for his sense of humour, whereas another is liked because of his fighting ability. All the differences come together, however, to make a squad that has bonded and will go a long way to protect the welfare of each individual member.

Of course, soldiers cannot be made to like one another; who one likes is obviously a matter of personal preference. Yet, in elite regiments, there are several types of experiences, rituals and behaviours which tend to make the soldiers have some sort of empathy

Special Forces beach reconnaissance

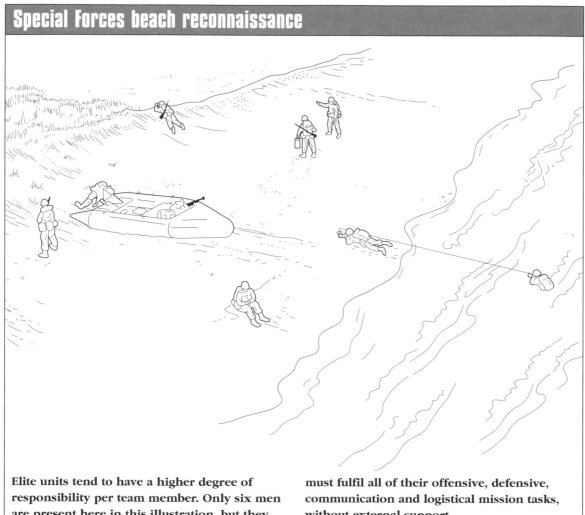

Elite units tend to have a higher degree of responsibility per team member. Only six men are present here in this illustration, but they must fulfil all of their offensive, defensive, communication and logistical mission tasks, without external support.

with one another, and this helps them to bond as a unit.

Belonging to an Elite

Just the fact that the soldiers are members of an elite force, distinct from the rest of the military world, tends to breed a greater respect for one another. The British Parachute Regiment, for instance, usually refers to all other non-elite regiments as 'crap hats'. This is no doubt offensive to those outside the regiment, but to those inside it signifies that they are special individuals who have a duty to protect the standards of the regiment and take pride in what they have achieved.

In both the British and US marines (and many other marine forces worldwide), once you have actually been a marine then you are 'a marine for life'. It is not uncommon for soldiers who left the marines decades previously and then who find themselves in trouble or facing hard times suddenly to receive support from the military fraternity who believes that being a marine means being accepted into a huge extended family for the rest of your life. Such a sense of belonging is one of the strongest forces for bonding men into a coherent team. This will express itself when entering combat.

Surviving Training

Elite training is an appallingly difficult business (attrition rates run at anywhere between 40 and 90 per cent). Just the experience of sharing the hopes and tribulations of basic training and coming through together tends to make soldiers connect with one another in a way that cannot be understood by many civilians. During Royal Marine training in Norway, all soldiers (except those over 30, who have the option of not participating) have to undergo a test in which they jump fully clothed through an ice hole into freezing water. Without any assistance, they must use their skis to clamber out of the hole. Yet once they are out, their fellow recruits will then set to work stripping them, drying them and putting them into dry clothing before hypothermia has the chance to take hold. Such is typical of the trust and intimacy that training builds up between the men. Furthermore, the process of training in elite forces is designed to weed out those individuals who have anti-social tendencies. Training effectively acts as a screening process for those who will not contribute to the team mentality.

Surviving Combat

As many war veterans have noted, sharing the experience of actual fighting can bring even the most ardent enemies together in a bond of friendship. Soldiers often report a sense in which the frustrations that tire most of us in civilian life suddenly seem totally irrelevant. Enmities and suspicions can be quickly forgotten and the soldiers have a common understanding which in itself breeds loyalty and a shared awareness of tactical performance. The writer Philip Caputo, a former combat officer with the US Marine Corps in Vietnam, recounts in his book *A Rumour of War* how two Marine soldiers were killed attempting to retrieve the bodies of fallen comrades despite their action almost guaranteeing their deaths. Such actions illustrate how combat and the esprit de corps can make the bonds between combatants extend even to those who are no longer living (it is part of the Marine code of honour not to leave the unit's dead behind on the battlefield).

Rituals

A final but far from unimportant element of team mentality is that of military rituals. The two most visible of these are ceremonies dealing with induction – particularly when a recruit passes training and becomes a full-fledged elite soldier – and ceremonies dealing with the burial of the dead. To take the latter as an example, prior to the American Civil War, the bodies of soldiers tended to be dispensed with little ritual and formality. More often than not, they were simply buried in ditches on the battle ground, left where they were to rot or given over to looters. However, from the later 19th century, the dead started to attract greater memorialisation. Monuments sprung up on battlegrounds – such as the monument on the Somme listing the names of 73,412 missing men – and, by World War II, cemeteries were created not only for the fallen of a particular nation, but also those of particular regiments and units. Most elite units today have some form of official cemetery and the often ornate rituals of burial give the regiments an intense feeling of pride in their abilities and sacrifice.

The factors which bring combatants together as a team in a military unit are many and are difficult to quantify. We have already noted four elements – belonging to an elite, surviving training, surviving combat and rituals – which help produce the correct commitment to the greater unit. So what type of qualities should the archetypal squad member demonstrate? After answering this question, we shall proceed by looking at how team-centred attitudes actually express themselves in the tactics and methods of combat. For, in the final analysis, military teams are created for fighting.

THE ELITE TEAM MEMBER

Returning to the Korean War again, research was conducted into the personalities typically found within those fighting squads which had consistently demonstrated success in combat. As we would expect, there were certain types of attitude or outlook which did not fit into an efficient squad. Men who were fearful of combat tended to demotivate combat squads and place a drain on their morale; fear, like anger, can be contagious within a squad. Also, men who were paranoid or overly imaginative could introduce an unwelcome friction into already overstretched frontline units. The final type of personality to have a detrimental effect on combat teams was that with poor social skills. Antisocial or unwelcoming personalities tend to repel people and, in a combat squad, this meant that the lines of communication had a weak link, as other squad members were reluctant to associate with the difficult person.

Yet, when looking at what was the right type of personality, what tended to come to the fore was that the individual members of the squad had to share a significant amount in common to be most successful in combat. The good team member usually displayed an open, personable character underlined with a mental strength which was not easily disturbed by adverse circumstances. People tend to learn much of their behaviour from those around them, so a strong-minded individual produces the beneficial effect of inspiring others around him to emulate his qualities. Interestingly, squads also seemed to benefit from being composed of men who were of a similar social standing in life, presumably because they shared a common language about life and experiences. A third factor in the competent fighting squad was that, if the individuals tended to display more barracks-type discipline – such as keeping their quarters clean and organised, responding quickly to orders, maintaining high levels of personal hygiene – then this seemed to express itself in a good fighting attitude.

An overall conclusion to emerge out of all studies into group behaviour in military units is that one bad apple can spoil the batch. During the Korean studies, good fighters were shifted together with other good fighters and these specially composed units were visibly effective in combat roles. Yet the more people the squad contained that were poor fighters, the more the efficiency of all the fighters was pulled down.

No Bad Apples

Here we are getting to perhaps the primary reason why elite forces are capable of such exceptional performance. Because training and standards are so high, there are in effect no bad apples. All elite soldiers are the best in their fields and thus the teams are consistently motivated to fight without reserve. Furthermore, studies since Korea have shown that, if a soldier feels himself a member of a prestigious team, he is capable of pushing himself to limits he would not achieve otherwise. A soldier who belongs to a team he is proud of is scientifically proven to be prepared to suffer more pain, more indignity and more suffering to maintain the welfare of the group than someone who is less committed to group thinking. Thus it is that all recruits to elite regiments are screened during training for their ability to

SAS 'Buddy-Buddy' system

The SAS 'buddy-buddy' system involves separating the men into pairs; each man in the pair looks out for the other, taking team trust to very high levels.

contribute to groups, rather than just their personal endurance or mental fitness. Essentially it is an issue of maturity. The soldier who keeps thrusting himself to the fore and taking charge may be eager to demonstrate confidence to his instructors, but the instructors may be more interested in the individual who is mature enough to step in and out of leadership roles according to the talents of the group.

By now, it will have become evident that being an elite soldier is about much more than just a tough attitude. Soldiers in units such as the SAS can be extremely individualistic, a tendency necessitated by the types of covert operation which are often pursued in isolation of human contact. Individualism, however, must not express itself as a lack of co-operative spirit, especially when it comes to the responsibilities of team operations.

THE FIGHTING SQUAD

Whether in the four-man teams of the US Marine Corps Force Recon or the 20-man patrol groups of the Italian Folgore brigade,

elite soldiers in combat formation rely on the team mind to form and apply effective tactical groupings. Perhaps the most obvious scenario for this is found in the work of the combat patrol.

Combat patrols come in many different shapes and varieties, but in terms of team co-operation, each patrol must have a similar set of priorities. First, the formation must allow quick and easy movement across the particular terrain. Secondly, the formation must present the squad's weaponry in its most advantageous configuration for both repelling attack and forming itself into a rapid attack. Thirdly, each member of the patrol must take responsibility for monitoring a certain sector of the patrol's aspect, each soldier adding to a 360-degree patrol observation effort.

One of the simplest formations is the six-man single-file patrol. This is ideally suited to covert operations in difficult terrains such as jungle, where the patrol may have to follow narrow tracks. The soldiers in this formation simply walk in line with about 3–10m (10–32ft) between each man. Although it seems a simple pattern, the teamwork to make this formation a strong one is considerable. The man at the front of the patrol – known in US circles as the point man – focuses his efforts in a 180-degree arc facing the direction of travel. His purpose is to pick up on any signs of enemy activity, watch out for booby traps or ambushes, and set the pace for negotiating the terrain. Behind him is the team leader. His role is not only to navigate the patrol (leaving the point man free to concentrate on his immediate environment), but also

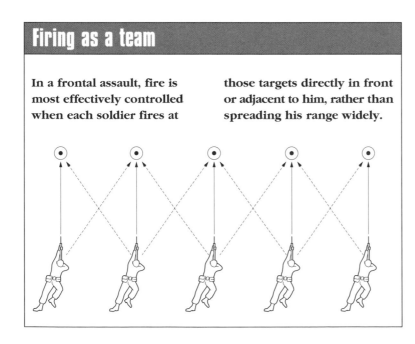

Firing as a team

In a frontal assault, fire is most effectively controlled when each soldier fires at those targets directly in front or adjacent to him, rather than spreading his range widely.

Team tactics in a river crossing

An advance party scouts the river bank and reports to the patrol. The patrol approaches the river using another route for extra security. One by one, the men of the patrol cross the river and those that are remaining act as a rearguard until they are all safely across.

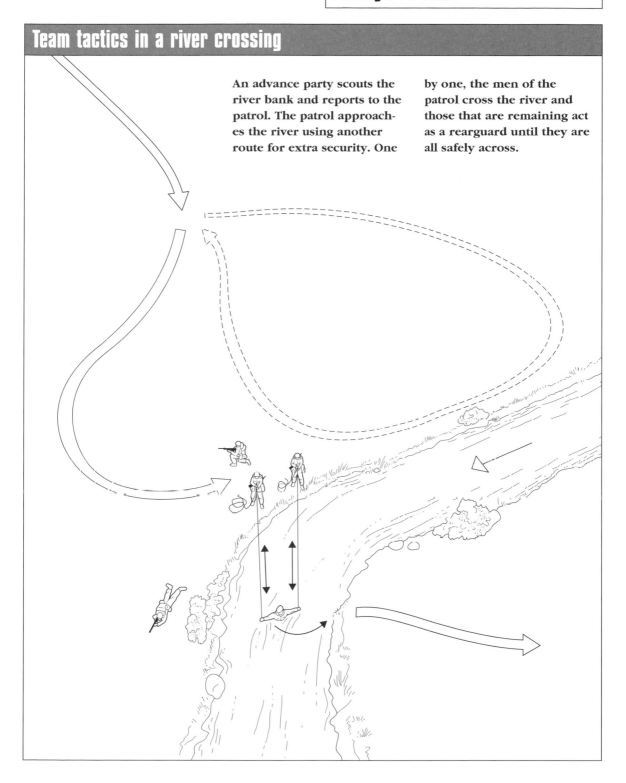

Milling

Used in the British Parachute Regiment, this tests recruits' resolve and builds team empathy. The soldiers box for two minutes, being scored on spirit rather than on blows landed.

to provide covering fire to the point man if necessary and take responsibility for monitoring one flank of the patrol.

The man behind him – the first flank scout – acts as a checker on the navigation and also tends to be the radio operator. He monitors the opposite flank to the team leader (the remaining members of the patrol alternate their flank observations, with the last member monitoring the rear so that the whole patrol is covered). Next comes the second flank scout, responsible for support weapons deployment and also acting as

someone who can keep the group together at the midpoint in night or low-visibility conditions. Finally, there are the assistant team leader and the rear scout, the former providing yet another check on navigation and also simultaneouly supervising the countertracking efforts of the scout positioned at the rear.

When analysed, what appears to be a simple single-file line of men actually turns out to be a highly organised formation with strict roles for each man. Mentally, the soldiers who make up this patrol must demonstrate several key qualities without which the patrol will be in a weak and vulnerable position.

Observation

Each soldier must take responsibility for his field of vision. This is an act of both discipline and trust. Discipline is required to keep the eyes working on your defined sector of vision, and trust is needed in order to be able to rely on the other members to do the same. Different methods have been tested and evaluated for heightening observation. At night, soldiers are trained to look at silhouettes, rather than stare into shapes, and they combine this with the use of the other senses to glean as much information from around them as possible. In jungle surroundings, the soldiers are taught not to focus on isolated features, but open what is known as 'eagle vision', where the peripheral vision is also engaged fully to make the soldier aware of movements or changes from any direction.

Reaction

In combat, a team relies on fast reactions from its members. All members of the patrol must hone their receptivity so that, should they spot a potential threat, they can convey the information to the rest of the team quickly and appropriately. For example, if ambushed, the team members of a four-man unit will have to react by establishing a surpressing fire from the middle two of the patrol, while the outer members advance and take the battle back to the ambushers. Unless this response is instinctive, it will be a weak one.

Communication

Although the physical act of talking or signing a message may not actually seem like a combat skill, it is paramount to the success of a squad in the field. Most elite training courses feature programmes in which the soldiers have to present formal lectures or presentations on a wide variety of military subjects. The purpose of this is to build up the soldiers' conversance with language, in order that they will be able to explain situations to others rapidly and accurately with a minimum of confusion on either side.

Weapons skills

Elite soldiers must be able to bring their weapons quickly into focus upon the enemy and deliver accurate fire. This is in itself a mental discipline. Calculations during the Vietnam War placed the average ammunition expenditure of US units for each kill scored at an astonishing 200,000–400,000 rounds. An elite squad must not waste a single round, for if one member of the squad expends his ammunition supply, then his place in the formation will subsequently become structurally weak.

On a typical mission, a special forces soldier will usually carry about 12 magazines for a weapon such as the M16. This is a maximum total of about 360 rounds, although extra loose ammunition will often be carried to replenish magazines. A 30-round magazine can be emptied from an M16 in about 3–4 seconds on full automatic, so elite soldiers rarely take their personal weapons off semi-automatic mode except for surpressing fire (full-automatic mode also has the tendency to result in muzzle climb and much-reduced accuracy). This restraint with ammunition is compensated for by exceptional marksmanship and targeting skills, and the elites' ammunition-to-kill ratio tends to be very low indeed. During contact between SAS soldiers and Iraqi troops in the Gulf War, even the SAS's belt-fed Minimi machine guns were only fired in three- to five-round bursts, although to stunning effect.

The file formation is only one example of a patrol organisation; others formations such as the spearhead and box formations are also used. Yet, regardless of the formation or of the purpose – whether they be ambush techniques, insertion patterns or open-battlefield units – the above principles of team support apply to all military groupings. Team co-operation enables elite units to form united firing positions at an instant and thus it gives them a force which often outweighs their numbers. During the Gulf War, for instance, a three-man group of US Special Forces soldiers around the village of Oawan al Hamzah was assaulted by Iraqi troops in large numbers. The situation was made even more acute by the fact that the US soldiers had only 300 rounds of ammunition between them. The group immediately fell into sensible and mutually protective positions and began a huge firefight. Unlike their adversaries, who had large supplies of ammunition and were pouring down fire on the US positions, the US soldiers settled into their positions and used single shots to pick off Iraqi troops, one by one. Through this tactic, plus the very brief use of automatic fire when their positions were immediately threatened, they succeeded in holding the superior forces at bay for a period of two hours. Eventually, US attack helicopters appeared and proceeded to lift them to safety.

The battle at Oawan al Hamzah illustrates that even a small group can have a great military effect on the course of a battle if its members think and act together as one. Indeed, it could be argued that team unity and motivation are perhaps the single biggest factors in the success of military operations.

When units lock together in combat, their primary purpose (alongside that of killing as many of the enemy as possible) is to impose such chaos on the enemy that its team structure disintegrates. There are many methods of doing this in battle. Using snipers to kill the enemy's officers is an excellent method of depriving an enemy team of its tactical direction (hence soldiers of special forces do not salute officers when they are on operations in order to avoid identifying their rank). Straightforward tactical outmanoeuvring is another method. This aims to turn the enemy team into a confused and disorientated outfit as they try to respond to a constantly changing battlefield. More broadly, enemy unity can also be assaulted through using various techniques of psychological warfare.

PSYCHOLOGICAL WARFARE

An example of this last form of warfare was conducted by Algerian insurgents during the war against the French which took place between 1954 and 1962.

The French efforts at suppressing the insurgents were fairly crude and definitely controversial. The use of torture and casual execution of Algerians became commonplace in the conflict. It was noted that although 15,000 French troops died during the conflict, as many as 300,000–400,000 Muslims were killed before independence was granted to the state.

In many ways, objectively speaking, the Algerian insurgents had a more sophisticated programme of military action than simply producing numbers of fatalities, like the French. Their programme aimed to undermine French unity and morale, and it was caried out by a group within the insurgents who were known as the Service Psychologique du FLN. This group launched a three-pronged programme of mental warfare directed against the French armed forces.

Firstly, they targeted efforts into bringing the civilian population onto their side, either through propaganda or through tricking them into participating in terrorist meetings or acts, after which the civilians were then obliged to continue working in the terrorists' pay.

Secondly, but related to the first point, the Service Psychologique du FLN directed their ambushes and bombings exclusively against

Areas of fire

Each of the patrol members in this team has responsibility for an angle of fire, adding up to a complete protective circle thrown around the entire group.

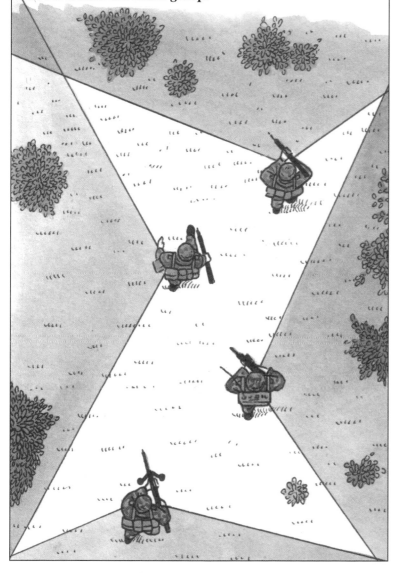

Thirdly, the group promoted their cause abroad, representing their efforts to foreign governments and pressure groups. In this way, they were to make the French actions of torture and execution seem all the more excessive to the outside world. (Ho Chi Minh in the Vietnam War applied similar strategies). This last form of action made many frontline French soldiers feel devalued and was effective both in sapping their morale and leading to several tactical and disciplinary problems.

The tactics used by the Algerian insurgents to attack the unity of the French cause can be equally applied by special forces soldiers as they conduct their operations against a wide variety of enemies. The key point to bear in mind is that once team unity has been destroyed, the enemy can then be dominated with much greater ease than they could have been previously.

The challenge for elite forces is to maintain not only a level of skills much advanced over that of regular forces, but also to create units which are capable of operating as a single fighting body in combat situations. In these units, every member understands his role and capabilities. To be a member of such a team requires character, humour and a certain willingness to contribute to something larger than you as an individual.

the military. This had the effect of chipping away at French morale, while simultaneously managing not to alienate civilian groups.

CHAPTER SIX

Leadership

Leadership is a vital component of a fighting unit's success. In the early hours of 19 July 1972, residents of the port of Mirbat in Dhofar province, southern Oman, awoke to the sound of gunfire. Underway was an attack by 250 Adoo insurgents against an SAS-led group which numbered only some nine men commanded by Captain Mike Kealy.

What followed was an astonishing defensive victory on the part of the SAS and an astonishing act of leadership by Captain Kealy. Captain Kealy's actions in the battle included instantly bringing mortar fire to bear on the attackers, racing through machine-gun and shellfire to keep a 25-pounder (11.3kg) artillery weapon in action, co-ordinating aerial bombing, holding an ammunition pit and killing Adoo attackers in the process.

Further SAS reinforcements eventually arrived and Mirbat was held against the odds. Every SAS soldier there acted with astonishing bravery, but Captain Kealy illustrated some of the fundamental qualities of leadership that we will explore in this chapter. He responded quickly and intelligently to the attack. He had a full knowledge of weapons deployment, which he brought to bear against the Adoo. Communications were controlled so that the forces outside Mirbat had clear mission directions. He showed evident concern for the welfare of his men while demonstrating enormous bravery. For his actions, he was awarded the Distinguished Service Order.

Captain Kealy demonstrated the best of elite military leadership and it is these qualities of mind and body which military recruiting stations around the world attempt to spot in their hunt for successful officer candidates. Not everyone is fit to be a leader or commander of soldiers. Indeed, those leaders who are held up as examples to the rest seem to be as much a product of their natural character as their military training. A successful leader is a mixture of character and

Handling patrol formations

A military leader must be able to visualise manoeuvres in the abstract – such as this patrol route – but then transfer them through practical skills into a working tactic.

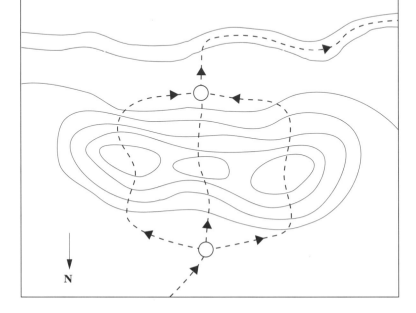

N

Leadership. As the title implies, the manual is intended for army officer instruction, but its principles are common to all services, including those of the elite forces (although differences will also be noted). It defines leadership essentially as 'influencing people – by providing purpose, direction and motivation – while operating to accomplish the mission and improving the organisation'. This, in turn, is boiled down to three key-words which must stand as the foundations of any military leader's success. These are 'be', 'know' and 'do'.

● **Be** – 'Be' refers to personality, having the character of a leader and exemplifying qualities such courage, loyalty and integrity. 'Be' also refers to having the necessary mental, physical and emotional skills to be able to command effectively.

● **Know** – 'Know' simply refers to knowledge, understanding the tools, tactics and organisation of a fighting unit so that they can be used intelligently.

● **Do** – 'Do' is the final part of the leader's initiative, when he takes his skills and character into battle and has to accomplish his objectives.

training, and, while the military establishment can provide the latter, the former is a much more elusive property.

LEADERSHIP AND CHARACTER

When talking about military leaders, it is usual to distinguish between being a 'leader' and being a 'commander'. Whereas a leader is someone who has the personality skills to make men and women follow him, a commander is someone who has the actual skills of directing people and machines in combat or another military situation. Only when personal and technical skills come together can the person be classified as an effective leader in a fuller sense.

This fact is recognised by one of the key publications on leadership, the US Army's Field Manual 22–100, entitled *Army*

Regardless of the military formation, we can see that these three elements must all be present for the leader to be a strong example to his men and a powerful force of guidance in action. First, we will look at the 'be' part of this equation, the character which the leader has which should separate him from those not suited to the nature of command.

Arguably, character is the most important element a leader brings to any elite force. An indication why this is so is to be found in the various mottoes which act as the moral standard for elite regiments. Such mottoes include (given here in English):

- **SAS** Who Dares Wins
- **US Marine Corps** Always Faithful
- **US Army Special Forces** Free from Oppression
- **Delta Force** Surprise, Speed and Aggression
- **Canadian Paratroopers** We Dare
- **Royal Netherlands Marine Corps** Wherever the World Extends

These mottoes vary in their emphasis, but what does not change is that each implies an exemplary standard of moral character to do the motto justice and to keep it respected. It falls to the officers to demonstrate the unit ethos to its fullest extent, so elite recruiters have a keen eye on who passes through their doors to see that they have the right character to stand as an example to the rest.

Each leader's character varies and, in a sense, there is no such thing as the archetypal leader. However, there are certain qualities which must be present for the soldier to function as a leader and offer the guidance and example required of his position.

Loyalty

A leader must show loyalty to his men, his branch of arms and his mission. If he does not give himself wholeheartedly to his unit, and remain unswerving from that commitment, the men under his command will not return that loyalty and so the efficiency of the chain of command will suffer and morale will weaken. Conversations with US Marines revealed that one of the greatest motivations behind soldiers' efforts was to justify their leader's trust, so in return the leader must show himself worthy of that position.

Personality characteristics in leaders

COMBAT LEADERS	GARRISON LEADERS
Mental composure	Sociable
Bravery	Meticulous
Aggressive action	Organised
Social tact	Highly motivated
Puts group before self	Self-restraint
Able to make rapid decisions	Disciplined
Confident	Intelligent
Able to inspire confidence	Versatile
Adaptable to circumstances	Able to discipline others with tact
Rapid thought processes	Strong communicator
Strong sense of humour	Understands people
Disciplined	Maintains high standards
Strong communicator	Able to juggle multiple tasks

Courage

Company grade officers – those who actually lead men into combat – have to possess the courage not only to deal with personal danger, but also demonstrate courage to their whole unit in order to inspire confidence. Courage should not be a blind force of will that overlooks the needs of the men. Indeed, modern military officers are taught to be very open to the welfare of the men under their charge. Instead, courage should simply be the resolve to hold to the mission's objective or the value of the regiment or unit in the face of adversity, without giving in.

Integrity

Respect for an officer must be earned – it is not something given automatically to the position. This respect is generally earned by consistently demonstrating the values of the unit and regiment, which in turn gives rise to an aura of integrity. The high value placed on integrity is suggested by the oath of office taken by commissioned officers in the US forces:

I [full name], having been appointed a [rank] in the United States Army, do solemnly swear (or affirm) that I will support and defend the Constitution of the United States against all enemies, foreign and domestic; that I will bear true faith and allegiance to the same; that I take this obligation freely, without any mental reservation or purpose of evasion, and that I will well and faithfully discharge the duties of the office upon which I am about to enter. So help me God.

The pledge which the US officers give is based on personal integrity, in which the soldier 'freely' commits himself to defending the values of his country and accepts

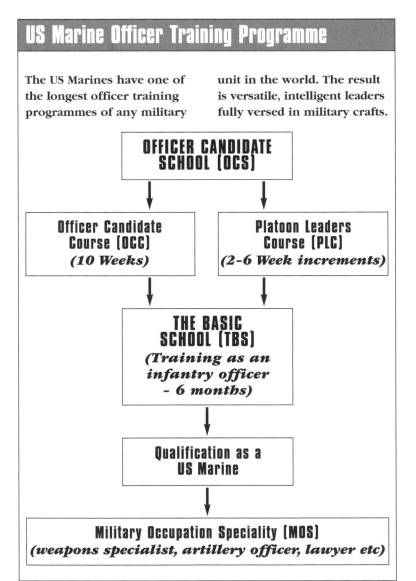

US Marine Officer Training Programme

The US Marines have one of the longest officer training programmes of any military unit in the world. The result is versatile, intelligent leaders fully versed in military crafts.

OFFICER CANDIDATE SCHOOL (OCS)

Officer Candidate Course (OCC)
(10 Weeks)

Platoon Leaders Course (PLC)
(2-6 Week increments)

THE BASIC SCHOOL (TBS)
(Training as an infantry officer – 6 months)

Qualification as a US Marine

Military Occupation Speciality (MOS)
(weapons specialist, artillery officer, lawyer etc)

the responsibilities of his position 'faithfully' and without duplicity. Military officers the world over take similar pledges to defend their own governments and nations.

Respect

General-Major Kurt Student, the founder of the elite German parachute regiments – the Fallschirmjäger – demonstrated the principle of respect as well as any other great military leader. During the early days of the parachute units, he used to give heavily of his time and energy talking to the men and discovering their concerns. 'During my frequent visits I made to the parachute units, I tried to set an example by talking to individual paratroopers, discussing their personal problems and eliciting their opinions. I was pleased with the way this approach was received, and there is no doubt that the parachute *esprit de corps* grew from strength to strength as the parachute corps expanded.' Although far higher in rank than the enlisted men, Student's evident respect for the opinions of those beneath him enhanced morale and also served to bond the paras to their leadership.

Student's approach to leadership is one endorsed by modern leadership training. Arrogance and dismissiveness are soon detected in would-be officers and, in most armies, these qualities tend to preclude the man from an officer position. This is not only a moral choice. The opposite of respect is disrespect and, if an officer displays this towards his men, their willingness to perform for him will be based on fear, a weak motivator. Consequently, respect is essential to secure the best unit performance.

Self-Denial

Although of a higher position than the men below him, the officer is there to serve others, not himself. In combat and in the garrison, he must put the welfare of his men, his regiment and his country before that of his own. During the Falklands War, for example, officers of units such as the Parachute Regiment and Royal Marine Commandos had to ignore their own exhaustion at the end of punishing marches to make inspections. They also had to ensure that the men were properly fed and that adequate foot care was being pursued to stop the onset of trench foot, a condition which afflicted many during the conflict. By serving others first, not only did respect for their position and natural authority build, but the chain-of-command was also able to operate at its full efficiency.

Apart from loyalty, courage, respect, integrity and self-denial, there is a whole range of other qualities that the officer must bring to his position. These qualities include self-motivation, enthusiasm, a sense of humour and a mind for detail. Yet there is no

Respect

It is possible to impart instruction and to give commands in such manner and such a tone of voice to inspire in the soldier no feeling but an intense desire to obey, while the opposite manner and tone of voice cannot fail to excite strong resentment and a desire to disobey. The one mode or the other of dealing with subordinates springs from a corresponding spirit in the breast of the commander. He who feels the respect which is due to others cannot fail to inspire in them regard for himself, while he who feels, and hence manifests, disrespect toward others, especially his inferiors, cannot fail to inspire hatred against himself.

**Major General
John M. Schofield**
Address to the
United States Corps of Cadets
11 August 1879

US Marine Infantry Officer Course

The pie chart illustrates the breakdown of IOC training, clearly illustrating the priority of field training in the US Marines.

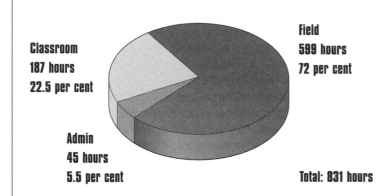

Classroom
187 hours
22.5 per cent

Field
599 hours
72 per cent

Admin
45 hours
5.5 per cent

Total: 831 hours

rule book, athletic, possessed of a passion for detail, had a good physical bearing and personal tact. None of these [qualities] was found to be relevant for an officer to be effective as a leader in wartime.'

So what are the marks of a strong and capable combat leader? Leadership in any walk of life is demanding, but there are surely no greater tests of command skills than those to be found in the chaos and horror of a violent military action.

THE COMBAT LEADER

The extent of a military leader's authority is exceptionally broad. Within the barracks alone, an officer will have responsibility for the organisation of his unit, the receipt, distribution and maintenance of equipment, unit accounting, and administration for food, clothing, accommodation, transport, health and welfare, discipline, pay, promotions and leave. As if this were not enough in itself, the officer also has to prepare himself for the experience of leading men into combat.

Under fire, a leader has to cope with enormous levels of distraction. Modern theory of warfare recognises that chaos is the primary ingredient of battle, with the situation shifting from one second to the next according the manoeuvres and casualties. A combat officer has not only to cope with the violence of the battle around him, but also to try to make tactical decisions in the midst of explosions and the dead and injured.

Producing the chaos-proof leader is never easy and training must be hard, realistic, pressurised and stressful to test who has the mettle. In the US Marine Corps, the officer

set formula for how each individual officer should actually behave, because that alters with different roles and different services. Officers in the SAS, for example, require fewer disciplinarian skills because the soldiers under their command are almost always highly motivated and self-disciplined. Thus it is that SAS soldiers and NCOs tend to call their officers 'boss' instead of 'sir'. Discipline is assumed, and being in such a close working relationship with individual men means that SAS officers have to have excellent interpersonal skills to gain the respect of some of the world's best fighting men.

Peter Watson, in his seminal book *War on the Mind* (London: Hutchinson; 1978), also investigated the difference between garrison and combat officers. Looking at studies done on company grade officers in the 1950s, Watson found that, while good garrison leaders 'were found to be aggressive, as were combat leaders [they] were also found to do better if they were sticklers for the graduate is meant to emerge with a clearly described set of skills and aptitudes, these being applicable to most elite units throughout the world. The officer has to be a:

- leader/commander
- decision-maker
- communicator
- warfighter/executor
- lifelong student of the art of war

Similar skills are also set out by the US Army's manual of leadership, in which four main sets of skills are set down:

- interpersonal
- conceptual
- technical
- tactical

Although the two lists use very different language, they actually share the same principles. Foremost among these is the act of communication. This is not just about the act of giving orders. Orders are a primary part of the officer's communications, but in addition to that is the two-way communication that sees the officer actually listening to what soldiers are saying. Good listening skills are required to absorb all the relevant information, respond to it and make the men feel that their contributions are valuable. Listening skills have been described as 'staring with the ears' and should place the emphasis on letting the person talk without interruption and without the listener constantly thinking up the next point of speech.

When an officer does speak, the voice should be clear, the language plain and easily understood, and the message should communicate the officer's high standards.

Major Qamar Hasmain's advice for giving orders

- Use a clear and firm tone that is easily heard and understood.
- Address the order to a very specific person or group of people.
- Be precise about what it is you expect the soldiers to achieve.
- Give few orders to avoid confusion and make sure that each is intelligible.
- Only give realistic orders in order that the soldiers can be reasonably confident about their achievability.
- Orders should be justifiable in the context of the situation or battle.
- Set down a proper timeline for the accomplishment of the order.

Furthermore, as some 70 per cent of the total message a person receives from another comes from non-verbal communication – body language, in other words – it is especially important that the officer projects physical strength and stature. A strong voice and strong body posture are taught on the parade ground, but their application is equally vital on the battlefield. In addition, the officer should also be able to change the mood of his voice so as to be able to deal with civilian presences on the battlefield, including those of children and old people.

While this accounts for the 'interpersonal' aspects of leadership skills, of equal importance is obviously the officer's knowledge of the tools of war: technical skills. In a modern military unit, the officer has tremendous resources of firepower on which to draw. A field officer in the 82nd Airborne Division, for example, may have at his disposal in a major action a company of troops armed with their personal M16A2 assault rifles, M60 and SAW machine guns, TOW, LAW and Dragon anti-tank rockets, mortars, Stinger anti-aircraft missiles, close-air support consisting of Cobra, Apache and Black Hawk attack helicopters, and howitzer artillery support. Co-ordinating such immense destructive potential on the battlefield is only possible if the officer understands the limits and applications of each weapon, and is also capable of orchestrating the communications technology that will bring all this firepower together. Added to this is the fact that vehicles such as tanks, jeeps and logistic trucks must also be harmonised behind the combat effort.

If the officer has a true grip on the equipment at his disposal, and also keeps himself up to date with new technology introduced into his unit, only then is he able to exercise possibly the most important element of a combat leader's ability: tactical skills. All tactical thinking comes from what is referred to in the US Marine Corps as 'decision-making' and what the US Army calls 'conceptual skills'. During officer training in most armies, officer candidates are put through a series of decision-making and tactical exercises which develop the individual's skills in responding rapidly to fluctuating situations or seemingly insoluble problems. In the British Army, for example, officer trainees are often given a piece of rope, a couple of oil drums and some board, and have to use these tools to cross a fast-flowing river – all done, of course, against a fast-ticking clock. The aim of the exercise is to see how these potential leaders can handle the realities of decision-making when the pressure is on.

Of course, the pressures of actual fighting are far greater than those encountered in the exercise just described. To attempt to simulate the reality of tactical decision-making, officers are tested in major field exercises during which they become accustomed to live-firing co-ordination. The exercises are valuable because, with powerful ordnance being used, the consequences of incorrect thinking could result in a loss of life as real as on the battlefield itself.

Barrel challenge

British Army officer candidates have often been tested by this: get yourself and your colleagues across a fast-flowing river using a barrel, some planks and a length of rope.

Once the officer candidate emerges from his training, he should possess the correct technical knowledge, decision-making skills and mental composure to be able to make tactical choices on the battlefield. The US Army defines tactics as 'the art and science of employing available means to win battles and engagements'. Yet here one of the key differences between elite and regular units emerges. The officer of a regular army unit may have his tactical focus set on the use of long-range weaponry, such as that commonly used in the Gulf War. During that conflict, tank commanders in US Abrams tanks would often engage the enemy vehicles at some 2700m (9000ft), in many cases out of range of the naked eye. For artillery and aircraft assaults, the ranges would be much greater. Without sight of the enemy, the tactical deployment of such weapons could be dispassionate and clean. Yet for elite units such as counterterrorist groups, the tactics revolve around the immediacy of human-to-human contact. Prior to the assault by troops

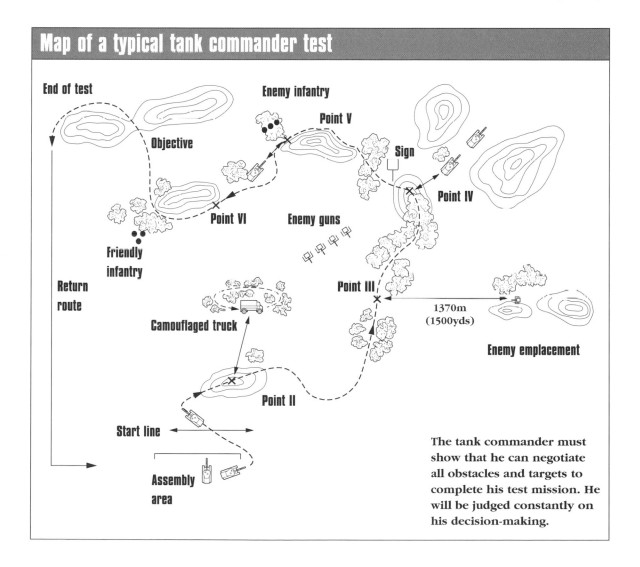

Map of a typical tank commander test

End of test

Enemy infantry

Point V

Objective

Sign

Point IV

Point VI

Enemy guns

Friendly infantry

Point III

Return route

1370m (1500yds)

Camouflaged truck

Enemy emplacement

Point II

Start line

Assembly area

The tank commander must show that he can negotiate all obstacles and targets to complete his test mission. He will be judged constantly on his decision-making.

US Marine decision-making

All US Marine soldiers are taught an effective method of decision-making which helps them to cope with the chaos of war and the constantly changing circumstances. It is called the 'Rule of Three'. When faced by any situation, the Marine soldier should define the problem as clearly as possible and then produce three possible courses of action. Any less than three and there are too few genuine options; any more than three and the soldier can become paralysed by indecision. From these three options, the soldier must choose one and then execute it vigorously. The overall result of the 'Rule of Three' is to give each soldier a decision-making method that avoids confusion and muddied thinking.

Unit allegiance

Special Forces take a unique pride in their regimental badges. It is up to the officer to act as an exemplary model of unit values and discipline while being an effective and humane leader of men.

of the German anti-terrorist squad, GSG 9, against the hijacked Lufthansa airliner set down at Mogadishu (the capital of Somalia) in 1977, the leaders were faced with tactical decisions of the most pressing kind. They would be attacking an aircraft isolated on a runway, containing four terrorists, 86 passengers and five aircrew. The terrorists' threat of blowing up the aircraft hung over every move. Somehow the GSG 9 operatives (and two SAS soldiers lent by the British Government) had to board the plane, take

out the terrorists and protect the hostages, all within the confines of an aircraft fuselage.

The plan was eventually put into action at 0205 hours on the morning of 18 October. A small fire was lit just ahead of the plane. This acted as a distraction to the terrorists, who had not noticed the elite troops mount the wings of the aircraft and move into position. At 0207 hours, the GSG 9 soldiers blew off the aircraft's emergency doors with explosives and stormed inside while throwing stun grenades and killing three of the terrorists

SAS battle – Mirbat

The map shows the flow of the battle, including the routes taken by men such as Kealy who demonstrated the SAS's core values of initiative and bravery.

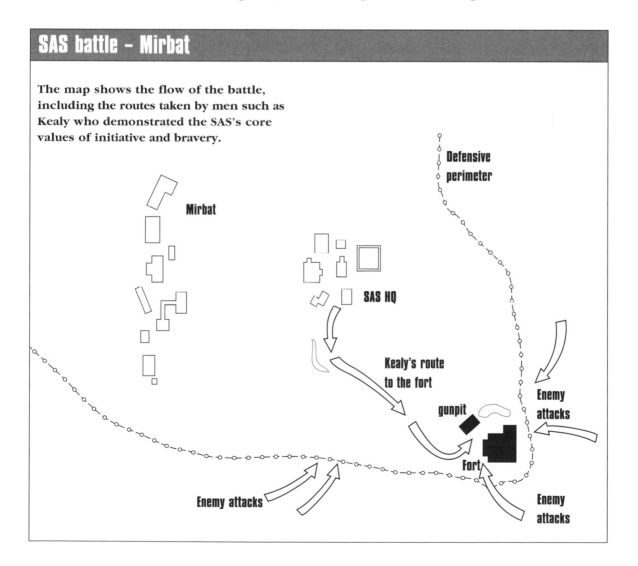

Mirbat

Defensive perimeter

SAS HQ

Kealy's route to the fort

gunpit

Enemy attacks

Fort

Enemy attacks

Enemy attacks

Academic learning

Officers must posses a high degree of technical, historical and military knowledge to be competent leaders. Classroom learning adds a vital complement to their field skills.

and wounding the fourth. The operation was a stunning success (only three hostages were wounded, none killed) and GSG 9 achieved the same notoriety in Germany as the British SAS would achieve in the United Kingdom after the Iranian embassy siege.

The Mogadishu rescue shows the tactical pressures faced by the officers of the elite forces. Their operations are often judged in a matter of seconds, rather than the week-long schedules of major warfare, and so they must show two primary qualities. The first of these is an intense attention to preparation, making sure that everything and everyone is in place before an operation begins. The second is that they are so well trained that they respond instinctively to the second-by-second developments of the action

itself, as conscious thought processes are just too slow. Elite officers do spend time doing rigorous and slow tactical planning, often using the 'sand table' technique of old (effectively a sand-covered war games table on which the tactical elements of the forth-coming battle are plotted). Yet equal, if not more, amounts of time are spent honing their skills under conditions of chaos and change, which is what they will actually face in the heat of battle.

PRACTICAL LEADERSHIP

Under the 'do' principle outlined in the US Army leadership manual, there are three categories of action listed which the leader should attempt to fulfil in his actual performance. These are:

- influencing
- operating
- improving

Influencing means that everything the leader does in action imparts a positive influence over the men under his command. During his training, the officer himself will have learnt much from wanting to emulate the officers above him and earn approval. Part of every officer training the world over is time spent listening to the stories of seasoned field officers. By giving accounts of their experiences in battle, experienced officers not only give valuable tactical lessons to the junior officers, but also act as examples which can inspire and motivate the junior officers during training. In the same way, the junior officers will then go out to their first command hoping to inspire confidence and determination. By influencing the men through example, and also through positive leadership skills such as communication and tactical awareness, the leader will aim to instil the motivation that leads to exceptional performance in the field.

When it comes to actually operating in combat missions, the true leader must control the process of battle deployment from beginning to end. Once he has received his mission, he must first begin the process of operational planning. Planning and preparation for battle involves several key actions which must be directed towards the central goal of using, in Clausewitz's words, 'physical force in order to compel the other to do his will'. Planning is a massive topic in its own right and could occupy an entire book (it is covered in more detail in the next chapter). However, a common way in which officers are trained in planning and preparation is to use what is known in military language 'reverse planning'. As its name suggests, this is based on defining the end result you are looking for from the action and then working backwards in time and

filling in all the stages required to meet that objective. Once you have worked back to your starting point, you have a complete plan for the mission.

Ceremonial duties

An officer must oversee ceremonial events and combat and garrison duties which are central to building up a strong esprit de corps within regiments and squads.

Any officer must also be aware at this stage of all the minor logistical needs that could upset his actual combat action. During some of the early campaigns in the Pacific during World War II, the US Marine Corps found that soldiers landing on the ferociously defended beaches of Japanese-held islands were running out of ammunition and had no adequate resupply. The problem, it emerged, was that ammunition was all too often stacked behind other supplies on the logistics ships waiting out in the bay. Thus the planning had to be readjusted so that officers consciously made sure that ammunition was placed at the front of the landing craft during the boat-loading phase of the operation.

As this example demonstrates, a good combat officer does not just focus his attention at the battle itself, but also on all the pre-battle factors that will exert their influence once battle has begun. An ideal way of ensuring that everything has been thought of, if there is time to do so, is to rehearse the action mentally from opening shots to completion. By doing this as realistically as possible, and building in some contrived disasters, the officer will reveal errors and problems without the life-or-death consequences of real battle.

Once the officer is actually in battle, the sum of his training, experience, planning and character will come into effect. The actual tactics of combat are covered in more detail later in this book. However, in summary, the officer in charge of a unit at the front during a battle must try to retain a close grip on the facts of the unit situation as it shifts and changes with the context of the fighting. If a machine gun jams, the officer must be aware that this is the case and alter his immediate battle plan accordingly. If he is wounded, he must have already made plain the mission's intentions to his subordinates. If the enemy suddenly capitulates, he must respond to the need for controlling prisoners and processing intelligence gained from the battlefield. Yet, while the status of the battlefield will shift from minute to minute, the officer must make sure that he keeps his attention firmly locked on the final objective. He may well be the only guiding force for his men, so, if he loses his sense of direction or purpose, then so will his unit.

Problem-handling

Leaders develop their subordinates by requiring those subordinates to plan. A lieutenant, new to the battalion staff, ran into a problem getting all the resources the unit was going to need for an upcoming deployment. The officer studied the problem, talked to the people involved, checked his facts, and generally did a thorough analysis – of which he was very proud. Then he marched into the battalion executive officer's (XO's) office and laid it all out in a masterly fashion. The XO looked up from his desk and said, 'Great. What are you going to do about it?' The lieutenant was back in a half-hour with three possible solutions he had worked out with his NCOs. From that day on, the officer never presented a problem to any boss without offering some solutions as well. The lieutenant learned a useful technique from the XO. He learned it so well he began using it with his soldiers and became a better coach and mentor because of it.

An example from the
US Army Leadership Manual

Sand-table exercises

The sand-table is an age-old method for officers to hone their tactical skills and decision-making. It provides more three-dimensional awareness than flat paper.

Even when fighting is actually finished, the combat officer's job goes on in improving the efficiency of his unit for when they next go into combat. Tactics, people, weaponry and the enemy must be rigorously and honestly analysed after the battle. The results of this assessment will then be shaped into a programme of improvement that systematically drives out the weakening factors present in the unit or its individuals. It is often in this time of reconstruction that the true qualities of leadership are needed.

Physical posture

A strong physical posture is emphasised in military forces because it actually leads to greater confidence of mind and a feeling of self-worth.

Many studies of effective military leaders have found that praise motivates soldiers more than criticism, so the officer must be diligent in giving sincere commendations to any personnel who have demonstrated good performance. For those who have not, punishment may be appropriate. This must not be overdone, however, and should fit into a clearly established scheme of punishment that is understood by all and is seen as fair. However, in many cases constructive criticism may be all that is required, especially if the officer makes the third party feel that he has let himself, his unit and his officer down by his performance.

At the beginning of this chapter, I commented that officers were mostly born and not made. Training and leadership development can produce fine leaders, but they tend to build on the fact that the candidates have strong personal characteristics. Good officers are vital. The consequences of poor military leadership can be truly awful for those on the front line (as history has testified), so military selection now weeds out the most unsuitable before training even begins. Of course, leadership is not just confined to the officers and ranked leaders. During World War II, it was actually discovered that in many cases it was the NCOs

Technical awareness

Officers should possess above-average awareness of the tools at their command. For instance, a searchlight should be gradually angled away from an enemy position during an advance to hide the troops behind the light beam.

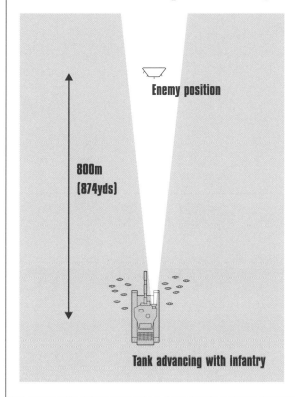

Enemy position

800m
(874yds)

Tank advancing with infantry

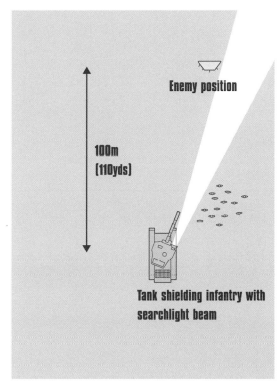

Enemy position

100m
(110yds)

Tank shielding infantry with searchlight beam

(non-commissioned officers such as corporals and sergeants) and even strong-minded privates which made up perhaps the most important layer of leadership. NCOs act as the intermediaries between the officers and the rest of the men. As such, they play a vital role in sustaining the emotional and physical welfare of the men. The NCOs also have to bear the brunt of training new recruits in the art of war.

Whatever the position within the unit, leaders must essentially exhibit the self-belief and confidence that enables them to make sound decisions and make others take up those decisions as their own. Leadership is a constant learning experience and decision-making ability does not grow overnight. This is recognised in the Marine Corps axiom that all Marines should be 'Lifelong students of the Art of War'. Marines are required to read incessantly on military issues and study accounts of battles ancient and modern. In this way, their understanding of war grows and thus so does their potential for being good leaders. Whether they have achieved such a status can only be tested in the front line.

CHAPTER SEVEN

Battle Tactics 1

Handling Major Manoeuvres

Once all the training is done, the elite soldier is left with the final test of combat itself. This is the defining examination of the soldier's mental stamina, personal courage and military expertise. Psychologically, his training will stand him in good stead, yet there are many things which he will only discover about himself once he actually begins to both face and deliver death.

This chapter is about how the mind applies itself to tactical combat, particularly on major missions where the fighting can be heavy (more covert operations are dealt with in the next chapter). As we shall see, the pressures of battle are intense because they draw heavily on both intellect and emotions, often in situations where the two are pulling against one another. The US soldiers who walked into the storm of fire at Omaha beach during the D-Day landings had to face a situation where to stay where they were would result in almost certain death, yet to leave their cover positions seemed to imply the same. Theirs was the challenge of battle, which is possibly the toughest psychological situation that any human being can face. Here, we will look more closely at this challenge and see how the elite soldier puts his mind to tactical situations to make him a truly formidable fighting force.

WARFIGHTING

There are few better interpretations of the nature of modern warfare than that found in the US Marine Corps' doctrinal manual, *Warfighting*. This was written in 1989 by the Marine General A. M. Gray as an attempt to define the principles of marine warfare in the context of modern fighting conditions. The manual defines the way a soldier should think about combat and how he should respond to it. Although it was written specifically for the US Marine Corps, its lessons have spread around the world to many military units and it will influence thinking about combat for many years to come.

Warfighting begins with a definition of war itself. In short, war is a chaotic and changeable situation characterised by traits such as 'uncertainty', 'fluidity', 'disorder' and 'complexity'. A military unit may hold clear objectives and focused targets, but General Gray states that once the enemy is actually engaged, unpredictable human factors come

Combat intelligence

In this illustration, a soldier places a pole charge. His application of this weapon means that he is enabled to employ a large destructive force with the minimum risk to his own safety, as he remains behind stable and solid cover.

into play and the situation becomes muddied and constantly shifting. Psychologically, therefore, the challenge for the elite soldier is not necessarily to impose order upon this nervous state of affairs (General Gray states that this is an impossibility), but to perform well, despite the chaos and the friction. This is an amazing burden and one which needs incredible qualities of character to handle it.

PREPARATION

Some battles are lost in the mind even before the first shot is fired. This is usually because either the soldier's morale is weak or the preparation for battle has been inadequate. Actually, these two factors feed off one another; weak preparation tends to result in a lack of confidence. Planning a battle or

special action is an incredibly difficult and demanding process which requires every ounce of a soldier's mental skills. Preparation is the first stage in overcoming the chaos of war and as such it is vital.

The penalties of poor preparation for military encounters are written in blood throughout history. For example, on 5 September 1972, eight Arabic terrorists of the Black September gang burst into the Olympic village in Munich, killing an Israeli wrestler and his coach, and taking nine other Israeli athletes hostage. German police units were put into action to retrieve the hostages, despite the fact that they were not properly trained for the role. They also turned down assistance from Israel's elite Sayeret Mat'kal counterterrorist unit. The police group decided that the best plan was for police

General Gray on war

War is characterised by the interaction of physical, moral and mental forces. The physical characteristics of war are generally easily seen, understood, and measured: equipment capabilities, supplies, physical objectives seized, force ratios, losses of matériel or life, terrain lost or gained, prisoners or matériel captured. The moral characteristics are less tangible. (The term 'moral' here is not restricted to ethics, although ethics are certainly included, but pertains to those forces of a psychological rather than a tangible nature.) Moral forces are difficult to grasp and impossible to quantify. We

cannot easily gauge forces like national and military resolve, national or individual conscience, emotion, fear, courage, moral, leadership, or esprit. War also involves a significant mental, or intellectual, component. Mental forces provide the ability to grasp complex battlefield situations; to make effective estimates, calculations, and decisions; to devise tactics and strategies; and to develop plans.

Although material forces are more easily quantified, the moral and mental forces exert a greater influence on the nature and outcome of war. This is not to lessen the

importance of physical forces, for the physical forces in war can have a significant impact on the others. For example, the greatest effect of fires is generally not the amount of physical destruction they cause, but the effect of that physical destruction on the enemy's moral strength.

Because it is difficult to come to grips with moral and mental forces, it is tempting to exclude them from our study of war. However, any doctrine or theory of war that neglects these factors ignores the greater part of the nature of war.

USMC, *Warfighting*, pp.15-16
(US Government, 1997)

Weapon control

A soldier should be so familiar with his firearm that it is an extension of his own body. Such familiarity will pay off in increased first-round kills on the battlefield.

sharpshooters to kill the terrorists as they crossed the tarmac at Fürstenfeldbruck Airport to a waiting Lufthansa Boeing 707 which was provided seemingly in compliance with the terrorists' escape plans.

Everything about the preparation was wrong. The snipers had single-shot bolt-action rifles unsuited to the demands of the mission; there was not enough illumination at the site; lines of fire were not judged correctly; there was no back-up force; and faulty intelligence had put the number of terrorists at four when there were actually eight. The

tragic consequence of this inadequate preparation was that the first volley of sniper fire only killed one terrorist. There ensued a four-hour battle in which the Israeli hostages were slaughtered and aircraft were destroyed by terrorist hand grenades. Only when the army was deployed was the situation brought under control, by which point the Israeli military leaders were openly crying with frustration and anger. Germany did learn from its mistakes; the truly elite GSG 9 antiterrorist squad was formed in the wake of Munich. However, the example does serve to show how, for military-style operations, those in charge of preparation must have the skills of mind and experience to judge what is needed and what may go wrong.

There are many mental ingredients to planning a military operation. Perhaps the primary of these is the skill of organisation. For a military force to be effective, its actions and its logistics must be organised properly from top to bottom. At the top level, there is the problem of co-ordinating supplies, transport, weapon supplies, fire support, delivery and extraction methods, food, relief and tactics. This requires a mind that can work from the smallest detail to the biggest picture and see how the two relate to the final objective. At the other end of the scale, each individual soldier must be able to accept responsibility for organising his own preparations for battle. For example, when looking at the Spetsnaz soldier and his equipment, the

diligence required in putting together such a kit is exceptional. Even straightforward items such as the AKM assault rifle require proper pre-operation maintenance, correct ammunition supplies and a full cleaning kit to be a sustainable field weapon. Add all the other bits of kit – including highly technical ones such as the anti-tank missile launcher – and the elite soldier has to have very good concentration and an established packing routine to ensure that he goes into action with everything he needs to be able to use his weapons.

Of course, organisational planning is shaped by tactical planning, and it is here that the mental abilities of the officers and NCOs really come into play. Returning to *Warfighting,* the manual gives us a soldier's perspective on the psychological traits required for designing tactics and effective combat plans:

Observation in urban combat

Placing himself low to the ground, the soldier can look round the corner with less risk of quick returning fire; the enemy expects a head to show at a higher level.

The Marine Corps' style of warfare requires intelligent leaders with a penchant for boldness and initiative down to the lowest levels. Boldness is an essential moral trait in a leader for it generates combat power beyond the physical means at hand. Initiative, the willingness to act on one's own judgment, is a prerequisite for boldness.

USMC, Warfighting, p. 57

The 'boldness' to which General Gray subscribes is something which enables a leader to design tactics that are shocking to the enemy. This is the hallmark of elite forces' thinking. If you go against an enemy with conventional tactics, the enemy will quickly grasp your intentions and react accordingly. Thus what you must do is design a method of combat that overwhelms the enemy's expectations and puts him in a continuous state of disadvantage.

Like the act of organisation, tactical planning requires the mental ability to juggle many considerations. Take as an example a theoretical raid on an enemy border post. The list of

Field targeting

By using a simple 180 degree clock system, the soldier can roughly identify positions to his colleagues. The point straight ahead is called 'axis of arc' and 45 degree to either side is called respectively, 'quarter left' and 'quarter right'.

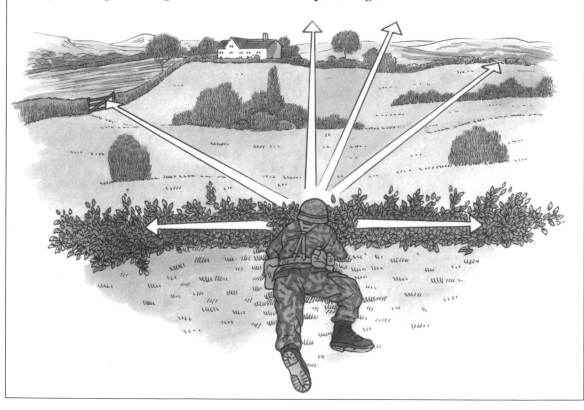

Urban combat firing positions

A soldier should select his firing position according to the following criteria: a) to reduce his silhouette to the barest possible minimum; b) to provide solid physical protection; and c) to allow the maximum arc of fire for his weapon.

considerations for such a mission is truly enormous and would fill a book of its own. Just a few of the issues at stake would be:

● How is it best to insert the attacking unit bearing in mind that the approach ground is scanned continually by thermal imagining cameras, motion-sensor equipment and dog patrols, and the approach air corridors have advanced radar surveillance?

● What is the strength of the enemy at the site? This includes manpower, experience of troops, weapons available, state of readiness and proximity of reinforcements.

● How is the border zone structured to generate maximum confusion once the attack occurs? How will the enemy troops respond once the firing starts and what are their positions of strength?

● Who are the best people for the mission within the units available? What is the status of their training, availability and experience?

● How will climatic factors affect the nature of the deployment, either to advantage or disadvantage?

The list of questions could go on and on, and it is imperative that the tactical designer comes up with satisfactory answers to each before the mission can go ahead. However, the tactical designer will also have to build in contingency plans should the mission not go as expected. In constructing the final plan, there are several criteria the planner must follows. The missions tactics must be:

Coherent

A tactical operation must be understandable by all involved and not be confused as to the objective or procedure. By ensuring this, the

Special forces ambush tactics

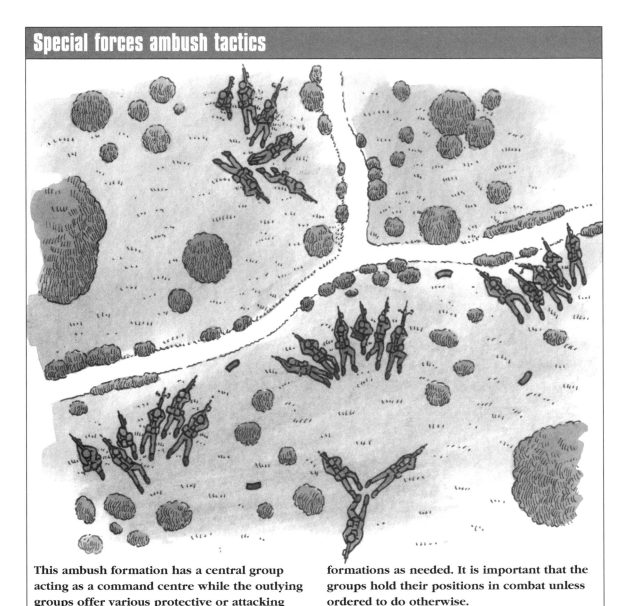

This ambush formation has a central group acting as a command centre while the outlying groups offer various protective or attacking formations as needed. It is important that the groups hold their positions in combat unless ordered to do otherwise.

leader knows that every man will be clear about his role in the operation and thus be able to give his maximum contribution.

Achievable

All military plans involve an aspect of daring and, in the case of special forces operations, this is especially so. Yet, however risky a manoeuvre, all soldiers must set out on their mission knowing that it is achievable, if only at the extreme. If a mission appears almost

suicidal in nature, the motivation of the unit will tend to be low, as the individual skills each soldier possesses will feel largely irrelevant. Instead, the operational plan must have a definite programme of deployment, objective and withdrawal that emphasises survivability as much as boldness.

Daring

In balance with the last point, elite forces' missions must have a dash of daring about

The V-shaped ambush

By adopting two arcs of soldiers in mirror image, these soldiers are able to ambush an enemy whose direction of travel is not known.

Because of their formation in these arcs, the soldiers are able to spread their fire across a wide area of attrition.

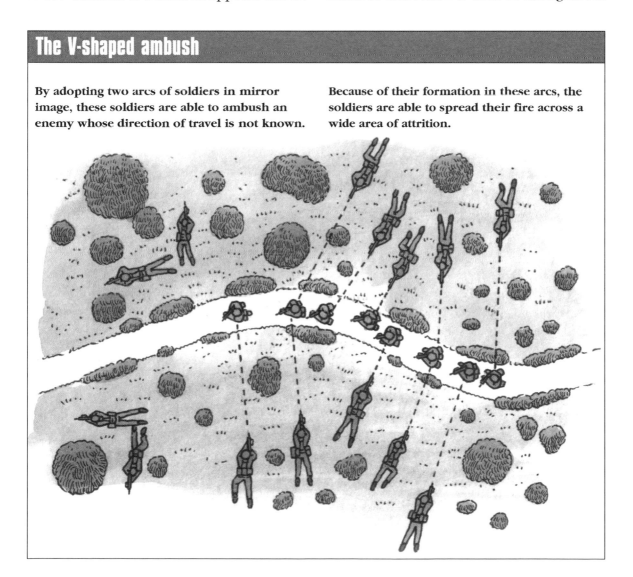

them. This is not simply for the pride of the unit, though doubtless that is important, but innovative and daring plans also tend to disrupt the enemy's defence by giving them a less predictable enemy to fight. A good example would be the SAS's raid on Pebble Island airfield during the Falklands War. Pebble Island acted as an air base for Pucara ground-attack aircraft; the aircraft had to be destroyed if the subsequent assault on the Falklands was not to be hampered. The SAS did this with great vigour, moving in under an offshore barrage from HMS *Glamorgan* before hitting the Argentine garrison hard with M203 grenade launchers, 66mm LAW rockets and 81mm mortars. Under this cover, an SAS assault team physically planted explosives on each aircraft to ensure destruction. By the time the raid was over, the entire Argentine garrison had been defeated and six Pucaras, four Turbo-Mentors and a Skyvan transport aircraft lay wrecked on the airfield. The mission illustrated how an attack of unexpected daring threw the enemy into total disarray and gave the elite forces a mental edge over their rivals. No SAS soldiers were lost in the mission.

Violent

If the mission is a destructive one by nature, the planning should result in a destructive force of great power being unleashed in a controlled manner. This principle can be applied defensively, as well as offensively. When Vietcong and NVA forces attacked US Special Forces camps in the Vietnamese highlands at places such as Plei Mrong and Nam Dong, they often found themselves slaughtered by US firepower despite being numerically superior. The Green Berets had set up interlocking defensive networks of machine guns, mortars, Claymore mines and assault rifles. During attacks such as that which occurred on 3 January 1963 at Plei Mrong, large numbers of attackers were hewn down by bullets, mortar rounds and

ball-bearings (from the Claymore mines) with appalling injuries. The successful defence of the camp proved the fact that firepower can be decisive when applied with maximum violence. The problems arise (as in the case of the Munich massacre) when weaponry is not intelligently used. Elite forces tend to be so familiar with weaponry that they do not overestimate the potential of firearms and thus plan weapon defences much more coherently.

Tactical planning is a difficult skill and it needs a great deal of confidence and vision to be done effectively. Not everyone is capable of assuming the responsibility, especially in life-or-death military situations, and some find it hard to live with the distinction between the clean ideas of the planning table and the bloody horror that results once their plan is put into life. However, what has emerged is that having someone detached from the nitty-gritty of the fighting is essential to the success of a mission. This is the role of the officer who is not actively present at the site of combat.

Information coming back from the battlefield tends to be very partial – soldiers see individual events before them and magnify them in their importance (although elite soldiers are trained in dispassionate observation). Thus, in World War II, it was common for infantry who had been attacked by tanks to report many tens of enemy vehicles when there were only a few. What a behind-the-lines tactician must do is interpret all the information coming to him from the battlefield and make cold decisions on a bloodless basis so that his judgment is not clouded by emotion (although he must remain sensitive to his men's welfare). Diagrammatic representation of the battlefield – such as the representation of the raid on a railway bridge – helps give the clarity of thought required when deciding on tactical advantage. It is this clarity of thought that should steer the action once the firing begins.

Anti-ambush measures

By nature, an ambush cannot be planned for; however, it can be controlled. This is done through utilising the correct formation. Here an ambushed party (top) make optimum use of a rearguard in order to perform a flanking retaliation.

THE MIND TO FIGHT

Those who have had to fight in actual combat missions describe a unique psychological experience. Many have described it as a sensation of 'hyper-reality' in which the experience of living under the incredible proximity of death and witnessing cataclysmic events makes the senses work unbelievably fast and ironically produces an incredible rush-like sensation of being alive and powerful. Such was described by SAS Captain Derrick Harrison during combat in France in 1944. Having driven into the French village of Les Ormes accompanied by a small unit of SAS troopers, he found himself faced by a truckload of SS soldiers. The firefight that broke out left him isolated under a hail of bullets:

I had grabbed my carbine and was now standing in the middle of the road firing at everything that moved; Germans seemed to be firing from every doorway. I felt my reactions speed up to an

Tactical challenges

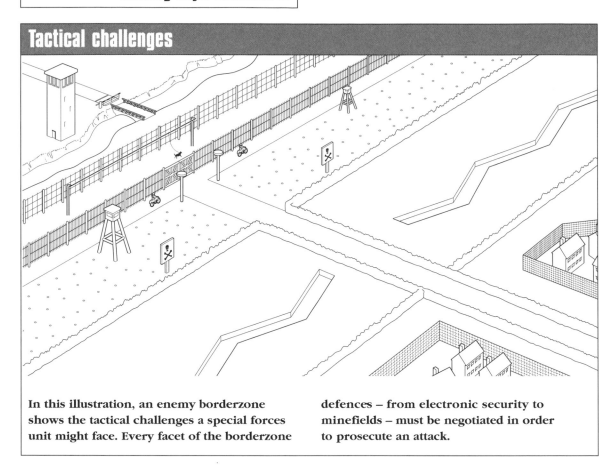

In this illustration, an enemy borderzone shows the tactical challenges a special forces unit might face. Every facet of the borderzone defences – from electronic security to minefields – must be negotiated in order to prosecute an attack.

incredible level. It was almost as if I could see individual bullets coming towards me as I ducked and weaved to avoid them. All the time I was shooting from the hip, and shooting accurately.

Harrison's sensation of 'speeded-up' reactions is a typical description of the way many soldiers feel in the height of combat. Modern psychology is indeed starting to reveal some of the basis of this response, often through the study of international athletes and disaster survivors. During extreme situations, the mind tends to adopt a tunnel-vision principle which focuses every effort on the act of survival or, in a military situation, on the act of either killing or avoiding death. This state of mind produces tremendous energy and mental acuity, and can often be the factor that decides whether a soldier lives or dies.

However, this is not all. Even in the fog of war, an elite soldier must draw on his training and mental discipline to think as clearly as possible in the circumstances. This is tactical thinking 'on the ground', the focus of the rest of this chapter. In making a shift from the tactical planner to the people who actually execute the tactics, we shall see how the elite forces training described earlier comes alive in practical decision-making on the battlefield.

INTO THE FIELD

Deployment is one of those times when nerves can be almost unmanageable. Sat in a helicopter or an APC, being rushed to a future that may be very short, the soldier can experience an overload of emotional demands at the very point where he should be thinking clearly. As we have already seen, however, there are steps that the soldier can take to control the anxiety. The first of these is mission focus – directing the attention entirely towards the mission at hand and mentally rehearsing the training and planning that has gone before. This has the effect of making the soldier more outward-looking and avoiding the introversion that leaves the soldier vulnerable to his imagination. Physically, deep, slow breaths will also help blood pressure and anxiety to fall to balanced levels. However, anxiety has a purpose in that it provides adrenaline for the demands of combat and so it is important not to push relaxation exercises to an extreme. As an old saying goes: 'It's OK to have butterflies as long as they are all flying in the same direction.'

If the soldiers are being deployed by helicopter into an isolated and uncontested area – such as British and US special forces were in the deserts of Kuwait and Iraq in the Gulf War – immediately after they are dropped at the landing zone, they tend to spend up to five minutes completely still and without talking to one another (if the situation allows). This serves several important psychological functions. First, it enables the men to adjust to their new environment and switch their minds from a training mode to a combat mode. Secondly, it helps their senses adjust to the sights and sounds around

them, especially after being in the noise and clatter of a military helicopter. This is particularly important if they are being deployed at night, as it gives them time for their eyes and ears to adjust to and process night-time sensory information.

Once this period is over, they can move out into their mission. At this point, the principles of co-operation and communication which were discussed earlier come into play. Each soldier must take charge of his role and communicate what he is doing to others, while making sure that he understands the function of each other member. Elite training is designed to make communication simple and practical in the field and thus remove the possibilities for misunderstanding. For example, when pinpointing targets or objectives to other soldiers, each man expresses the world in front of him as a semicircle divided into five axis points – left, quarter left, ahead, quarter right and right (see illustration). This can be indicated by hand signals if silence is nec-

Principles of tactical movement

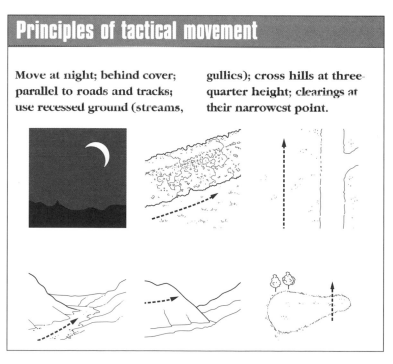

Move at night; behind cover; parallel to roads and tracks; use recessed ground (streams, gullics); cross hills at three-quarter height; clearings at their narrowest point.

essary and gives the soldiers the ability to target features with limited room for confusion. That way the group stays working with a shared understanding of both where they are and where they are going.

Raiding a railway bridge 1

A good example of tactical intelligence in action. The raiding party attack the bridge itself while two other groups deploy as protective elements either side of the bridge.

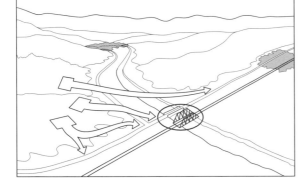

Raiding a railway bridge 2

Once the demolition charges are placed, the groups withdraw in two different directions in order to confound the tracking enemy forces.

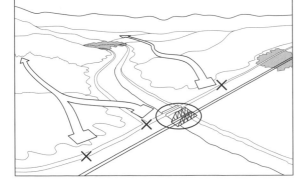

By communicating effectively, the team will have a clear understanding of where they stand in relation to one another and that builds confidence in the competence of the team. When moving into position, each team member must adopt a coherent position in relation to everyone else so that the group functions as a single entity. This is well demonstrated by ambush technique. The diagram nearby shows a typical special forces ambush in readiness to receive enemy soldiers down a rural track. The main attack and command element is set close to the track and will basically control the pace and tempo of the ambush, but these soldiers will also act as the guiding point of communication for the four security elements surrounding them as back-up. The virtue of this configuration is that the assault party can draw in reinforcements from any direction around them. Furthermore, the security troopers can also catch any escaping enemy soldiers in a vicious net of firepower, as well as protect the withdrawing assault party and fight off any enemy reinforcements who come to the scene. The important issue for when the ambush is sprung is that each soldier holds his position unless guided to do otherwise. The security troopers may be positioned some distance from where the main attack is taking place, but, despite their eagerness to enter the fight, they must not do so unless it becomes part of the group strategy as a whole. This example shows how self-discipline and team-mindedness are essential ingredients of any special forces squad, as each man has a dependency on the man next to him.

The example of an ambush also leads us to another factor of tactical and psychological performance that is crucial to the success of a special forces operation: fire control. Fire control covers the spectrum from the way a soldier uses his rifle in personal combat to the manner in which he brings in air strikes. The quality which should distin-

SAS tactics – Iranian Embassy siege

Note how the SAS team took command of the building from the top down. When attacking buildings, descent is always faster than ascent.

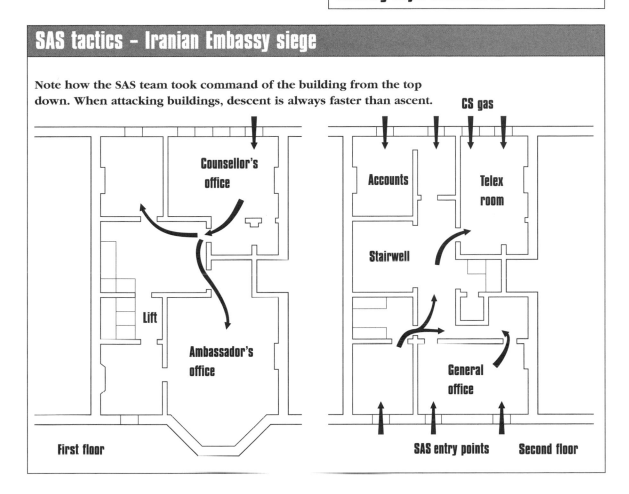

guish a special forces soldier from the rest is that his application of firepower is controlled and deliberate. We have already seen how ordered semi-automatic fire is often much more effective than heavy automatic fire at medium to long ranges. Special forces soldiers are trained to handle their rifles in a very conscious and aware manner. If faced by a large group of enemy soldiers, by far the most effective fire is delivered when a single individual is picked out at a time, aimed at and fired at until he goes down. Each victim is consciously selected, targeted and killed, this fire discipline resulting in a much higher percentage of kills than random, erratic 'spraying' and also conserving more ammunition. It was such a style of weaponcraft that confused Iraqi soldiers over SAS unit strength in the Gulf War – they could not quite believe that so few men could injure the large numbers of their soldiers dropping from gunshot wounds. Elite soldiers also tend to pick their targets more intelligently. Killing an officer or a radio operator creates greater confusion in the enemy camp than simply shooting a regular foot solider; putting an LAW rocket into a truck's engine or communication equipment starts to impact on the enemy's logistical capabilities.

Controlled firing requires a disciplined mind in the furore of combat and an in-depth

British tactical questionnaire (1940s)

1) Why would you avoid a skyline when acting as a scout?
2) What sort of background would you choose if exposed to view in sight of the enemy?
3) What is the reason for track discipline? What is revealed by aerial photography?
4) Why is the time factor so important in war? Can you give an example of its value?
5) When is the best time to attack parachute troops? How are they armed?
6) What is the distinction between parachute troops and airborne troops?
7) How are parachute troops trained?
8) What is the spearhead of a German panzer division?
9) Why cannot chemical fire extinguishers be used to put out incendiary bombs?
10) Give some examples of good camouflage.
11) What is the purpose of Axis propaganda?
12) What is the meaning of total war as practised by Germany?
13) Do you know any rules of war as recognised by civilised nations?
14) When is it particularly advantageous to use hand grenades, bayonets?
15) What equipment is used for crossing water obstacles?
16) What preparations would you make before starting a long march?
17) What action should be taken if a gas shell has made a crater in the road?
18) In which part of the sky would you expect to find the 'Great Bear'?
19) How could you conceal a loophole?
20) How might the concealment of a weapon pit be endangered?
21) What is the modern method of designing a fire trench?

perhaps the most psychologically cruel of all the warfare scenarios. It is apt to produce tremendous confusion, as attacks lose coherent lines and opposing forces mingle together. Fire can come from any direction and the effect of explosions is compounded by the enclosed spaces. Yet even in this environment, the special forces soldier can control his tactical movement by doing the following:

● Present as small a silhouette as possible. Urban landscapes consist of right angles; the human form stands out clearly when framed by the side of a wall edge or door. Thus, adopt firing positions at small apertures such as a hole in a wall and, when moving, try to stay parallel with a flat surface to confuse the enemy's eye (such as rolling over a wall).
● As the enemy will probably be at close quarters, know your next position of movement. A fixed firing position in urban combat is dangerous because of the risk of being outmanoeuvred from many angles. Grenades or rocket launchers may get a bead on you – the enemy can pinpoint your position to a certain window or doorway – thus, move intelligently to positions which minimise your danger, but put the enemy at a disadvantage.
● Hide behind structures capable of stopping heavy-calibre weapons. This is not as obvious as it sounds – .50 calibre machine-gun bullets can punching through concrete pillars and brick walls. Go for multiple-layer structures and angled features such as the corners of buildings.
● When crossing between points of cover, make the crossing as quick as possible.
● When looking around a wall, peer around it at a level close to the ground; an enemy watcher will not expect to see a head at foot height and this will delay spotting time.

knowledge of firearm usage and effects. The same discipline is also required in the art of tactical movement. Every act of relocation changes how much a soldier can see and be seen. The soldier's objective is to present as little of himself to enemy view while maximising his tactical advantage, meaning that the special forces soldier must be expert in reading terrain and position, and deciding on a course of movement before taking it.

The nature of tactical movement varies with the type of terrain. We will look at two types here. The first, urban environment, is

- Take a building from the top; moving down through it enables the attacking force to achieve greater speed and momentum. It helps with fire deployment, as grenades can be thrown down stairs; throwing them up stairs risks the grenade rolling back towards you.
- Select firing positions which present little of you to the outside world, but enable you to traverse a wide arc of fire. This principle has been applied for centuries. Archery holes on castles are often no more than a few inches wide, but have angled side facets to allow the archer to fire over a 90-degree radius.

Combat in a rural setting has different challenges. Principles of movement are based on presenting the slightest and briefest target possible to your enemy:

- When moving around a hill, loop around it two-thirds of the way up the slope; this allows you the quickest passage around it without exposing yourself as a silhouette at its crest.
- Avoid open ground, especially if framed by woodland or hedgerows. Use vegetation features as natural tracks for covered movement. Cross open ground quickly at its narrowest point.
- Do not use roads or tracks, as they are strong fields of fire and ambush. If you have to move up along a road, do so at either side of the road, where you are less visible (termed 'handrailing').
- If you are trained in countryside night fighting, use it; it will compound confusion in your enemy. .Principles of camouflage can be exploited in a countryside setting, but changing seasons require different colours (snow is an obvious example).

Whether operating in a city or in the countryside, such principles of manoeuvre will be second nature to a special forces soldier by the time he has completed his training. In combat, the mental blueprint of these tactical considerations should allow him to respond appropriately as a reflex action. Psychologically speaking, tactical combat skills enable the soldier to operate amid confusion and chaos with some degree of clarity. The principles of his training impose shape on a fairly shapeless scenario. Also, being conversant with tactically controlling chaos allows the pursuit of what the *Warfighting* manual terms 'maneuver warfare':

… a warfighting philosophy that seeks to shatter the enemy's cohesion through a variety of rapid, focused, and unexpected actions which create a turbulent and rapidly deteriorating situation with which the enemy cannot cope.

USMC, Warfighting
(US Government; 1997), p. 73

Not only is the special forces soldier intended to increase the level of control over the battlefield, but also at every level to inflict snowballing degrees of chaos on the enemy. The aim is to attack the parts of the enemy's psychology and physical strength that result in that enemy's collapse as a coherent force for fighting.

The manual goes on to highlight the main areas in which this can be achieved: focus, the aggressive focus from when the point of attack is decided and the full force of arms is brought against it; surprise and deception, highlighting the importance of doing what your enemy does not expect; and shaping the action, encompassing a range of tactical actions such as judging the enemy's overall composition and understanding his surfaces (points of strength) and gaps (points of weakness). By understanding both of these, you are able to control the action by directing your efforts against the enemy's gaps, and in this way destabilising his entire system.

CHAPTER EIGHT

Battle Tactics 2
Counter-insurgency

Counterinsurgency forms perhaps the most significant operational profile of most elite regiments. Termed variously 'low-intensity conflict', 'guerrilla war' and 'terrorism', this half-war of violent struggle is not an engagement of major armies using instruments of mass destruction (although conflicts such as Vietnam show us that can be its outcome).

N or is counterinsurgency predominantly fought by conventional soldiers with regular soldiering skills. Instead, the new way of war is the conflict which sits awkwardly somewhere between civilian and military struggle. It features sporadic acts of violence – the car bomb, assassination or ambush –

often propagated by an unseen enemy who shrinks invisibly back into the populace after each attack.

The new war requires a new breed of soldier. Insurgency has to be fought by soldiers who can actually insert themselves into a foreign society – either as combatants or as

Watch navigation

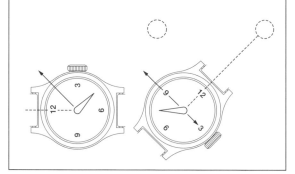

In the northern hemisphere bisect the angle between the hour hand pointing at the sun and the 12 mark to give a north-south line. In the southern hemisphere point 12 at the sun.

undercover operators – and use all their skills to unearth this enemy from within. The skills of counterinsurgency are the focus of this chapter. Yet, rather than exploring the minutiae of counterinsurgency applications, we will reveal the exceptional personal qualities a man or woman should possess to make the ideal antiterrorist fighter or agent. Counterinsurgency, as we shall see, demands possibly the greatest level of intelligence, creative thinking and self-control of all military roles. Those who execute its undercover missions are some of the world's most talented military minds.

THE ENEMY WITHIN

The postwar military situation is unique in that the war against terrorism has taken an equal priority to the conduct of major military operations by regular armies on the battlefield. Yet this is not to say that guerrilla warfare – fighting conducted by irregular forces outside of standard acts of engagement – is a new phenomena. Indeed, the opposite is the case. Small-scale terrorist attacks go back to ancient times, when indi-

vidual Roman soldiers died as a result of furtive stabbings when on guard duties in the Empire's far-flung Middle Eastern and southern European colonies. Still, many military analysts have defined the true birth period of guerrilla war as the late 18th and early 19th centuries. What changed was that insurgency became an actual way of war, rather than something incidental to a larger conflict. At this turning point, we see 'guerrilla' actions such as the Vendée uprising in France (a revolt by people in western France and Brittany against the revolutionary government) and the attacks by Spanish insurgents made against Napoleonic French troops in Spain from 1807. In fact, this latter conflict spawned the term 'guerrilla' itself, the translation 'little war' indicating the difference from the usual conflicts of massed armies and open battlefields.

It was exactly the massed armies' inflexibility and massive inertia in movement which the insurgents sought to exploit. More and more nationalist and politically motivated groups were finding that an apparently smaller, weaker force could take on a far greater military unit if it did not fight on conventional terms. From the early 18th century, guerrilla-style warfare spread across the world to become more of a deliberate tactical choice. France would endure many more periods of violent insurrection following the Franco-Prussian war. Italy spawned guerrilla heroes such as Guiseppe Garibaldi, who fought against Austrian power in Italy. In the US Civil War, bands of Confederate insurgents attacked Union troops in the Shenandoah Valley. At the end of the 19th century, British troops clashed in the African Transvaal and Orange Free State for almost two years with the unpredictable and fast-moving horse-mounted Boer irregulars.

The 20th century if anything increased the pace of guerrilla conflict, especially as movements became increasingly tied to new political philosophies of Marxism and revolutionary theology. From 1916, the British struggled with Irish independence movements, a bloody beginning to a terrorist war which has lasted to this day. Arab insurgents conducted campaigns against the Turks between 1916 and 1918, a conflict which involved the famous participation of Captain T.E. Lawrence ('Lawrence of Arabia'), who later wrote on guerrilla warfare and declared that 'granted mobility, security, time and doctrine, victory will rest with the insurgents'.

Lawrence's comments are evidence that, by the early decades of the 20th century, guerrilla warfare was entering a kind of tactical respectability and, indeed, the 20th century saw perhaps the fullest flowering of guerrilla warfare. This was particularly so with the end of World War II, as many nations such as the United Kingdom, Portugal and France struggled to hang onto their crumbling colonial power in the postwar era. Colonial conflicts led to the greatest proliferation of guerrilla warfare, particularly in the Far East and Africa.

However, conflicts such as those in French Indochina between 1946 and 1954 and the Congo in the 1960s were also shadowed against the international backdrop of the Cold War. The Soviet and NATO superpowers may not have clashed directly during the tense period following World War II, but they expressed their political wills in small proxy wars around the world's battlezones. Their military sponsorship of various affiliated groups allowed guerrilla wars to grow into major outright conflicts – Vietnam being the classic example. Escalating from small guerrilla war to full-blown war, Vietnam showed the military world that counterinsurgency was perhaps the most difficult yet imperative role for its forces to assume. A nation like the United States found that, despite its unsurpassed might, the daily political and human consequences of sporadic shootings and ambushes added up to a wearing tactical quagmire.

Day/night vision

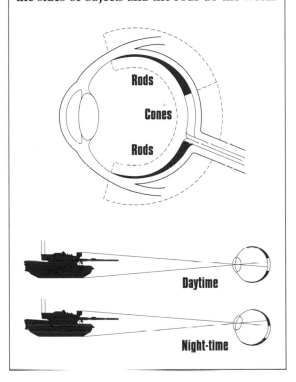

Light is projected onto the cones at the back of the eye; the peripheral rods become more sensitive at night, when the soldier looks to the sides of objects and the rods do the work.

Rods

Cones

Rods

Daytime

Night-time

That lesson stays with us. Although the Cold War is now over, insurgency flourishes all over the world, expanding with a variety of new themes and intentions. Although the communist and capitalist ideologies which fuelled actions in the past may have been replaced by religious and sectarian motivation, however, the horrendous effects of murder and bombing are still the same and governments are still destabilised by the slow and unpredictable grind of violence. It is little wonder, therefore, that counterinsurgency can perhaps be said to have become the dominant role for elite forces worldwide.

TERRORISM VERSUS COUNTERINSURGENCY

On many occasions, forming an effective military response to guerrilla activity has actually been the catalyst for the development of many of the world's elite units – for example, the re-establishment of the SAS during the Malayan Emergency of 1948–60.

The reasons why counterinsurgency so often falls to small, elite squads are many. Chief amongst these is the fact that counterinsurgency operations require a level of tactical sophistication and practical skills which would be impossible to transfer to large squads. A singular illustration of this was the

Walking at night

Walking silently at night requires that the soldier ensures that the foot is picked up high and placed down slowly. This is done by leading with the toe. True mental stamina is required to keep this up hour after hour and resist rushing.

Testing the ground

At night, a soldier must remain aware of possible booby traps. A soldier tests for trip wires with a wooden stick to avoid completing an electrical current.

role of the SAS in Malaya. Britain's efforts to quench the violence of the Malayan Communist Party (MCP) guerrillas not only included major regular army operations, but also sophisticated SAS missions in which the elite troops conducted social actions, as well as military ones. In 1952, the Military High Commissioner in Malaya, General Sir Gerald Templer, channelled more military energy into winning over the support of the common Malayans than was spent in trying forcibly to defeat the communists. This became known as the 'Hearts and Minds' campaign, a term which has grown in currency ever since. The SAS soldiers involved in the campaign had to mingle with the Malayans, learn their language and culture, and offer them friendship and support, as well as occasionally act ruthlessly against the

terrorists. By helping the locals, the British hacked away at the communists' social support base and left them more isolated and easier to target. Thus, when the SAS emerged from the jungles at the end of the emergency, many had acquired skills such as dentistry, building and midwifery, as well as veterinarian care.

The example of Malaya illustrates how counterinsurgency is a job requiring an above-average intelligence and a sophisticated approach to conducting campaigns without necessarily using violence. Yet violence is also required and counterinsurgency soldiers must also be trained to deliver that with brutal focus. Counterinsurgency is often the province of elite squads because terrorism is an innovative form of warfare and one which demands the constant upgrading of tactical skills. In Malaya and Vietnam, jungle-based counterinsurgency combat had to be perfected. From the moment Palestinian terrorists hijacked an El Al Boeing 707 from Rome to Algiers, counterterrorist forces had to develop tactics for dealing with the hijack of civil passenger aircraft. Embassy-based terrorism pushed the development of rapid building assaults such as those used by the SAS against the Iranian embassy in the 1980s. The use of bombs in urban settings – the most visible in recent years being incidents such as the bombing of the World Trade Centre in New York – necessitate against-the-clock reactions and also the ability to defuse ordnance. The list of counterinsurgency threats and countermeasures goes on and on, but what is evident is that the men and women given the task of working against terrorism in either aggressive missions or undercover work have to be the most highly trained in the world.

So what type of person do you need to be to fulfil this role? To answer that effectively, we need to see what the counterinsurgency soldier faces, and we can do this by stepping inside the mind of the terrorist.

TERRORIST PERSONALITIES

In recent years, the traditional profiles of the insurgent have dissolved. Whereas, in the 1960s, terrorists tended to be motivated by hardened political ideals, today's 'insurgents' can be anything from extreme Islamic guerrillas to isolated individuals who commit violence for reasons known only to them. Yet when the target is more military in nature – as in defined terrorist groups such as the IRA in Northern Ireland or the Basque separatist ETA in Spain, or the Vietcong in Vietnam – there does seem to be a typical group of characteristics or definitions.

Insurgents are recruited to the cause through a variety of routes: threats, bribes, promises of social improvements, or political ideals. In Indochina in the 1950s, the Viet

Minh would organise political rallies at which trained observers would monitor the crowd for those individuals who reacted positively to the message. These would then be approached after the meeting with a view to joining the ranks. Other recruitment strategies were less subtle. A common tactic used in Vietnam was for the insurgents to commit an action against US or ARVN forces, which in turn provoked retaliation against a certain village or district. The populace that suffered under this retaliation thus came to associate the US soldiers with aggression and violence, and expressed their animosity by becoming members of the Vietcong.

All recruits to an insurgent organisation tend to be 'loyalty tested' – made to perform some task which establishes their loyalty to the cause or puts them in an incriminating position. This testing will start simply and build up slowly, working from, say, the delivery of an apparently important letter to the receipt of illegal arms. Needless to say, the penalties for betrayal can be appalling. The Vietcong used tactics such as cutting open the 'traitor' and letting wild pigs eat him. Naturally, such horrific treatment brought in more totally faithful recruits through abject fear.

Recruitment of insurgents also tends to be focused on those individuals who are discreet. Like their elite opponents, insurgent organisations cannot work with those who will brag about their role in the struggle and thus reveal the operational workings. Recruits, therefore, might be tested by first being given a piece of seemingly vital but actually spurious information. They are then given the opportunity to reveal it (perhaps using an attractive member of the opposite sex to increase the desire to impress). Should the person reveal their information, they are ejected from the organisation, or worse.

Interestingly, when studies were conducted into what motivated terrorists in the Indochina and Vietnam conflicts, in the majority of cases, the simple desire to improve material wealth seemed to be dominant. Less than 40 per cent of Viet Minh captured in French Indochina actually proclaimed an acceptance of the communist cause. The rest were more inspired by the pursuit of greater wealth, which tends to explain why so many recruits to terrorist organisations come from disadvantaged backgrounds, particularly the rural working class. In the Korean War, 70 per cent of insurgents were labourers, farmers or peasants. Once inside the terrorist organisation, the individual is indoctrinated as to its values and beliefs, and they are also placed into its structure. Studies have tended to show that insurgents generally work in 'cells' of five to eight people – any less than five and individ-

ual personalities tend to become too dominant and any more than eight and the group tends to split into factions. Of course, there are exceptions to this. Mao Tse Tung constructed his guerrilla forces into squads of 9 to 11 men and these in turn into companies of 120. Yet, regardless of size, each squad tends to be assigned a distinct role. Thus, in organisations such as the IRA, some squads would work in an intelligence-gathering capacity, whereas others would function as assassination groups.

Becoming a full member of the organisation tends to involve initiation rituals of many types. These are important in that they give the individual a sense of belonging to his new group and also make him feel that he has achieved a special status within his

Undercover operator

A counter-insurgency soldier must consciously select the most inconspicuous routes possible to move around. Here a soldier uses a culvert to cross a road.

Watchtower attack

Guards are particularly vulnerable to fatigue and boredom, especially at night, when most special forces units will choose to conduct their attack.

The leader is usually the most publicly visible element of the group, but especially in the earlier stages of a campaign, terrorists tend to be almost invisible within their society. This is their source of ultimate strength. The advantages that insurgents have over their conventional opponents are extensive, but the key factors which make them so problematic to deal with can be listed as follows:

●**Freedom of movement**. Terrorists are not constrained by conventional patterns of strategic movement. During the Vietnam War, the threat from the Vietcong could emerge from almost any quarter, ranging from a bomb attack in central Saigon to an ambush in the mountainous Vietnamese jungles. Because insurgents rarely fight open battles, counterinsurgency forces face a difficult challenge in knowing exactly where they are and what are their tactical intentions.

society. Often the rituals will be in some way inspired by the words of the movement's overall leader – a very important figure for the insurgent. The list of leaders is extensive: Che Guevara for the Cuban revolutionaries, Mao Tse Tung during the Chinese Civil War, Ho Chi Minh for the Viet Minh, Osama Bin Laden for Islamic fundamentalists. Such figures give their groups a psychological cohesion and a figure who resolves disputes, gives direction and doctrine, and inspires.

● **Anonymity.** Insurgents rarely wear uniforms and tend to be fully integrated into their national society. This means that, unless they are caught in an act of terrorism or intelligence reveals them, their identity will be almost entirely unknown. Such anonymity gives terrorists the advantage of being able to select and observe prominent targets at leisure, and also to lull the enemy troops into a false sense of security by apparently offering them friendship and various services.

- **Social support.** Few terrorist organisations operate in isolation from significant levels of social support. Insurgents are not simply comprised of fighters, but also of an entire network of support from a willing sector of the populace who provide logistical, financial and operational assistance. During the war in French Indochina between 1945 and 1954, some 340,000 Vietnamese were members of the Village Militia, a grass-roots organisation of men and women aged 18–45 who rarely fought, but gave the logistics and intelligence for the Viet Minh to function as a truly effective fighting force. Breaking the link between the terrorists and their social support is a primary task of counterinsurgency forces.

- **Unpredictability.** Terrorism can be run with military efficiency, but more commonly it is a loose and unpredictable expression of violence. Sometimes terrorist organisations appear out of nowhere and commit horrific acts before melting back into obscurity. Terrorist leaders can often be psychologically unstable characters whose operations are conducted on the basis of whim and mood. Also, terrorist organisations tend to change shape rapidly, forming alliances and renaming themselves according to new goals. Such makes the movements of insurgents incredibly difficult to predict and pre-empt. Italy, for example, has an estimated 150 terrorist organisations living and operating within its borders, a presence which has resulted in a disturbing trend of murder and bombings over the past 30 years. Looking at the situation worldwide, whereas almost 80 per cent of terrorist violence before 1970 was expressed against property, since the 1980s that percentage has now been taken by attacks directly against people. Diverse organisations and shifting trends make it hard to pin the terrorists down to any single pattern of operational focus.

Against this backdrop of terrorist strengths, what can the elite counterinsurgency troops offer to control insurgency? The scale of the problem is massive – a study conducted in Tel Aviv found that only one in 10 terrorists is ever actually caught – and there are doubtless too few elite soldiers to combat such a worldwide phenomenon. Thus, police and security forces conduct most antiterrorist work. However, in certain instances, a more superior military presence is required and this is when the acute mental skills of the counterinsurgency fighter come into play.

THE COUNTERINSURGENCY FIGHTER

Elite troops tend to be employed for counterinsurgency in two distinct roles. One is in the scenario of urban terrorism, in which they are applied to hostage and building assault situations. The other is the deep-insertion mission, often in the context of serious rural terrorism. Here, the elite soldier is placed deep within the environment of the insurgent, acting either as a hidden combat presence, working undercover within the terrorist organisation itself, or taking an active role in building civilian resistance against the presence of insurgents. It is this second role that is our focus here, as it demonstrates more fully than most other circumstances the mental agility of the special forces soldier.

To look at the mental profile of the counterinsurgency soldier, we must examine the general skills of undercover operations used by elite soldiers and the mental intelligence that goes with them. Undercover operations range from reconnaissance within enemy territory to impersonating enemy personnel, and they are an extraordinarily demanding element of special forces work. First, we shall look at the essential combat skills of counterinsurgency and undercover operations, and secondly at the equally important and fascinating social skills required.

Combat Skills

The psychological challenge of undercover operations begins from the moment of deployment. For covert operations, night insertion is typical, often by parachute or helicopter. This presents its own set of mental challenges. If entering the contested territory by parachute, special forces often do so by one of two challenging methods of

parachute technique which bring their own psychological problems.

The first of these techniques is High-Altitude High-Opening (HAHO). With this technique, the parachutist is dropped some miles from his destination at an altitude of up to 7620m (25,000ft). The canopy is quickly deployed and thereafter the parachutist 'flies' silently to the destination in a shallow-angle drop which can last more than an hour and requires nimble steering.

By contrast, High-Altitude Low-Opening (HALO) parachuting sees the soldier dropped at a similar altitude or higher, though this time he freefalls for several minutes and only deploys the parachute in

HAHO parachuting

The parachutist is deployed from a high altitude, deploying his parachute quickly and fliying to his target many miles away. Mental problems: severe cold and oxygen deprivation.

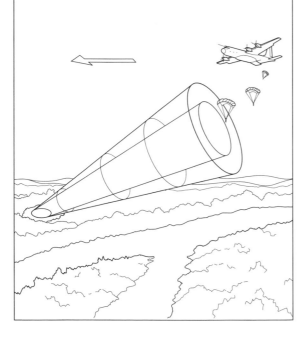

HALO parachuting

The parachutist is deployed from high altitude, but freefalls and opens his parachute in the last 609m (2000ft). Mental problems: timing must be perfect despite freefall disorientation.

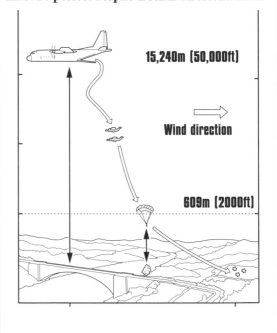

15,240m (50,000ft)

Wind direction

609m (2000ft)

the last 609m (2000ft) of the jump. This gives an extremely rapid deployment method.

Both techniques pose psychological problems. The oxygen levels at 25,000ft and over are very low indeed, and temperatures can be –50°F (–45°C). Lack of oxygen and severe cold can induce feelings of sluggishness, disconnection from reality, unconsciousness, confusion and blurred vision. All these are anathema to the sharp mind required at this dangerous moment of the operation, so enough oxygen should be carried on both types of jump in order to supply the soldier to beneath 3048m (10,000ft). Clothing should also be extremely insulated.

Landing in the operational area by parachute, or by the much noisier helicopter deployment, requires a switch of mind. Unless the situation demands it, the soldier should spend a few minutes still and silent in his new environment, adjusting to sights and sounds, and becoming familiar with his operational world. At night in particular, the soldier's senses are placed under acute strain. The human eye takes about 30 minutes to adjust fully from normal daylight to night vision, even longer if the soldier has been exposed to bright sunlight in the daytime (which explains why special forces soldiers in bright conditions tend to stay indoors or wear very dark sunglasses). This is

Underwater operations

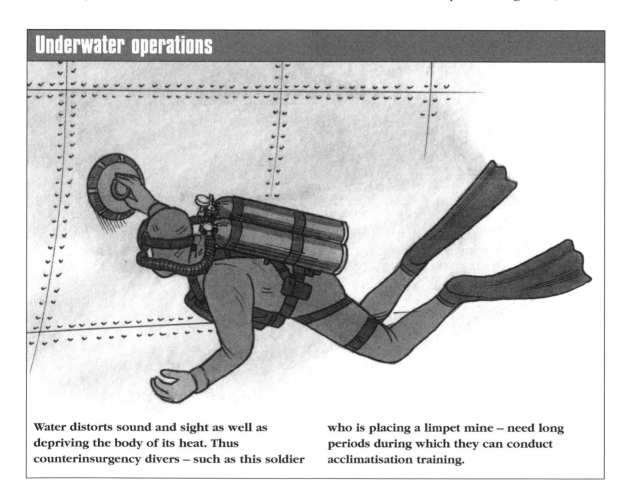

Water distorts sound and sight as well as depriving the body of its heat. Thus counterinsurgency divers – such as this soldier who is placing a limpet mine – need long periods during which they can conduct acclimatisation training.

Reading the ground

Undercover soldiers must become expert in 'reading' for signs of enemy presence. Footprints and litter can offer vital clues to enemy numbers and force.

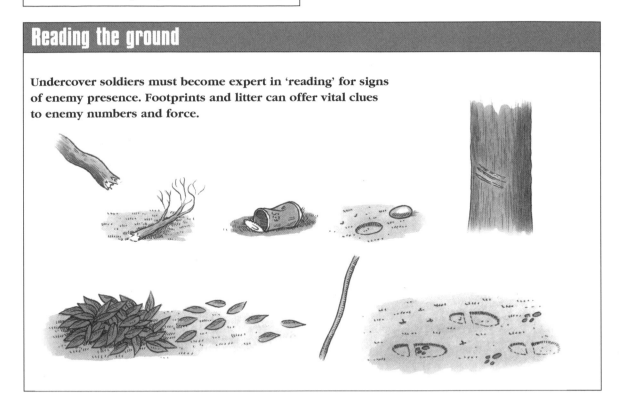

because at the back of the human eye are two types of cell: rods, which pick out the general shape of objects; and cones, which give more precise colour definition. Rods are positioned more peripherally around the eye, whereas the cone cells sit directly behind the retina. At night, however, the rods become more receptive to light. The effect for the soldier is that staring directly at the silhouette of a human figure at night results in the shape fading from vision, whereas looking to the side or above the shape allows the peripheral vision of the rods to work better and define the shape more clearly. In training for night combat, therefore, the elite soldier must practise shooting using peripheral vision, as looking directly at the target will usually result in the soldier shooting high. Instead, the gun should be pointed at the base of the target, trusting to the fact that the gun is actually on target. This is a difficult

mental skill to master and must be reinforced by continual night-firing exercises.

Once on the move at night, the soldier must bring all his other senses into play. Smell can give vital indicators of an enemy presence. Elite soldiers are taught to angle their noses 45 degrees to the wind and breathe slowly, but punctuate this with short, sharp sniffs to maximise their scent detection. When detecting noises, the head should be shifted from side to side to try to locate the exact position of the sound. Sounds directly to the front or to the rear can be misinterpreted for the opposite positions if there is no other sensory information. For this reason, head-turning is vital in order to gain a correct bearing.

When on the track of an insurgent or regular enemy, observation and memory are perhaps the two key mental qualities that a soldier must bring to bear. These two mental qualities feed off one another: observation builds clues as to the nature of the enemy presence and the memory enables the soldier to sort these into a meaningful pattern of behaviour of which he can take advantage. Observation is more of a skill than is first imagined. Every scrap of information must be taken in – colours, shapes, textures, movements, intuitive responses – and then assembled so that anything out of the ordinary is received and understood. In this way, the soldier is able to pick up on the signs of enemy presence.

Any indicators of enemy presence are known as 'sign' and are divided into four categories: ground sign (below knee height), top sign (above knee height), permanent sign (sign that does not degrade with the elements) and temporary sign (sign that does degrade with the elements). If his training is good enough, a simple sign such as a set of footprints should tell the soldier how many enemy passed that point, roughly how long ago, the direction of travel, whether any of the men had an injury and even whether the soldiers were carrying heavy equipment. Combine this with all the other available sign - such as disturbed foliage, human waste, discarded equipment – and the soldier is able to build up a strong profile of whom he is facing and also be aware of ambushes and booby traps.

Of course, the undercover soldier must conduct all his operations without being detected. This in itself requires great self-control and patience. For example, walking at

Footprints

Footprints provide the soldier with clues about the enemy. A moist, well-defined footprint is recent; the state of others can tell soldiers when the enemy passed.

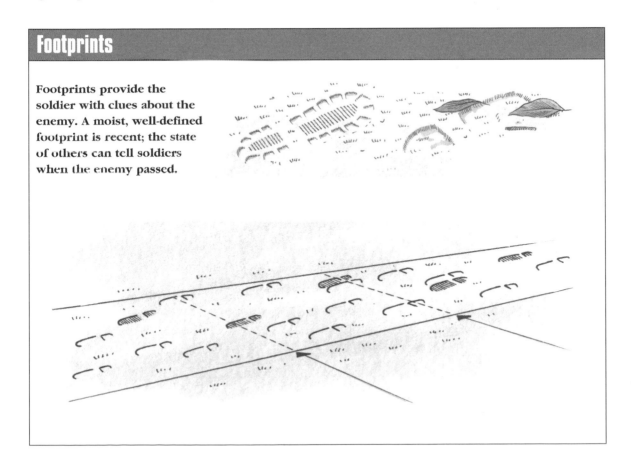

night requires that the soldier raise his knee high, place his toe down slowly onto the ground, then gradually roll the rest of his foot onto the ground to take the pressure. This movement is easy to sustain for a couple of minutes, but to do this hour after hour requires enormous self-discipline to resist the impulse to walk as usual and make greater speed. Similarly, covert surveillance positions are often cramped, damp and uncomfortable and, once occupied, physical strain and mental boredom must be dealt with. During training for the British Parachute Regiment, recruits are often given an exercise where they have to sit cross-legged facing a stone wall, all located on the summit of a bleak Welsh mountain. The instructors monitor the men for those who are unable to cope with the prolonged stillness and mental inactivity. Those who become agitated and restless would make

poor counterinsurgency, undercover or sniper soldiers, as such roles demand mentalities which can cope with little stimulus for hours or days on end, but then suddenly become alert and focused when the situation changes.

It will now be apparent that the undercover operative is a truly special individual who must display a formidable breadth of mental skills. During the 1960s, US Special Forces devised tests for the entry of its counterinsurgency soldiers. Psychologists at the US Army Personnel Research Office (USAPRO) conducted a varied and punishing range of tests which produced a list of eight psychological characteristics for counterinsurgency soldiers:

- resistance to mental and physical fatigue;
- ability to make decisions in fluid and unstructured circumstances;

Covert surveillance

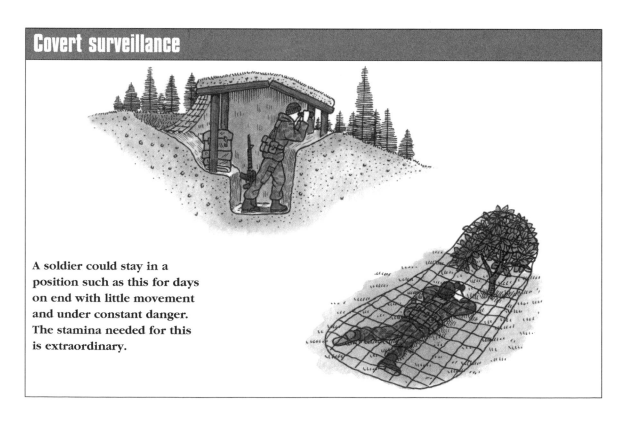

A soldier could stay in a position such as this for days on end with little movement and under constant danger. The stamina needed for this is extraordinary.

Remaining invisible

The undercover soldier must know how to detect the enemy but how to remain undetected. A trooper steals food, making sure he leaves no footprints.

- ability to operate as part of a team;
- ability to face combat situations with resolution, courage and tactical skills;
- ability to absorb and retain military information;
- the right frame of mind to treat training as real;
- ability to cope with missions in which the level of progress or the course of action is not known;
- acceptance of the training course as something which cannot be left voluntarily.

If the recruiters could find people with this distinctive mind-set, they could then produce efficient and dependable counterinsurgency teams to be left in the field for long periods without the weakening of morale or resolve. Of course, genuine and extensive combat skills were also required to cover all missions' outcomes, from pure reconnaissance to a major engagement with the enemy. In the early 1970s, the Human Resources Research Office (HRRO) conducted research at Fort Benning in the US and produced a list of areas of skill needed for counterinsurgency units (in this case labelled 'small independent action force', or SIAF):

- individual weapons
- explosives and demolitions
- hand grenades
- machine guns
- physical and mental strength
- using aerial reconnaissance pictures
- maintaining physical wellbeing
- tracking
- communications
- navigation

- using techniques of covert movement
- delivering artillery fire and air strikes
- setting and detecting mines and booby traps
- mountaineering
- survival, evasion and escape
- leadership
- tactical organisation
- first aid
- intelligence
- liaising and using air mobility
- using image intensification equipment
- applications for boats and techniques for river crossings
- applying sensors
- social missions, including the training of foreign troops

(For more details see Peter Watson, War on the Mind, *London: Hutchinson; 1977.)*

Hearts and Minds

A 'hearts and minds' campaign builds up the local civilian or military population to fight its own battle against the insurgents, either by direct military action or by depriving the enemy of popular support. The US 5th Special Forces Group (5SPG) in Vietnam created 42,000 Civilian Irregular Defense Groups (CIDGs), made up of Vietnamese soldiers who were persuaded to fight for the South Vietnamese cause against the Vietcong and NVA, capably adding to the South Vietnamese war effort. Living for long periods amongst the Vietnamese populace, the US soldiers picked up their language and customs, using them against the communists. Such talented influence has led elite soldiers worldwide since the Vietnam War to be trained extensively in these kind of techniques. Cultures can differ in extraordinary ways. Some cultures place a lower value on human life than Western cultures. Oriental cultures often give greater credence to unchanging nature, rather than human progress. In the Middle East, it is regarded as rude to talk about an important issue straight away. A social minefield awaits the elite soldier on a hearts and minds operation, compunded by the fact that he is usually trying to get a community or group to commit to patterns of behaviour which could place them under threat of violence. Training involves lengthy studies of the target culture and acquisition of the language. The soldier must develop:

Language skills

The soldier should be able to speak without preparation on almost any given topic without undue pausing or lack of vocabulary, switch between formal and informal forms of address and demonstrate competence in language-based intelligence tests.

Negotiation and Argument

The soldier should be able to reason and argue using the different conventions of the society for which he is destined. In any negotiation, the soldier must take into account religious standards, moral codes, styles of argument and whether decisions are made by groups or individuals. The soldier should be an adviser in the foreign group's midst, letting the decision-making proceed naturally.

Modesty

Recruiters have long avoided what they call the 'James Bond type', an individual who is attracted by the role of the undercover operator due to its status. Those who can carry out impressive deeds without confiding details to anyone are favoured. In the British Intelligence Corps, on a scale of 1 to 5, 1 is someone modest and stable enough to keep secrets without tension, and 5 someone who will talk too readily. Only people who score 1 or 2 enter the intelligence corps.

Impersonation

Soldiers working closely with a foreign culture must also be able to impersonate its

Observation

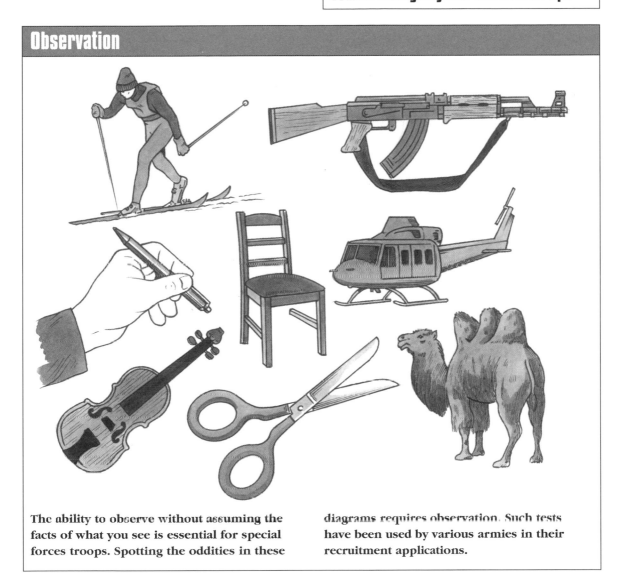

The ability to observe without assuming the facts of what you see is essential for special forces troops. Spotting the oddities in these diagrams requires observation. Such tests have been used by various armies in their recruitment applications.

physical mannerisms. For example, Middle Eastern peoples stand close to each other, using constant expressive body gestures to back up their speech.

These are just a few of the qualities that the counterinsurgency soldier must display during operations. If he can combine his combat and social skills with an understanding of his enemy, he will make an effective force against insurgency. He can create an environment of hostility which will control the possibilities of what the enemy can do. The intelligence and mental versatility of individual agents and soldiers, rather than large-scale manoeuvres, is essential. As terrorism and guerrilla war are increasing worldwide, elite soldiers will continue to receive training in the varied skills of this exacting form of warfare.

CHAPTER NINE

Detention, Escape, Survival

Elite soldiers are valuable assets worth preserving, and governments are keen to avoid their special forces falling into the enemy's hands. In terms of cash expenditure alone, each soldier of an elite regiment such as the SAS or US Marines, or specialists such as aircrew, has more money invested in their training than perhaps an entire squad of regular soldiers.

Add to this equation the fact that they are usually privy to some of the world's best-kept military secrets and it becomes apparent how desirable it is for the enemy to capture one of these personnel.

This is obviously easier said than done. Part of the training which elite soldiers receive is in the very tactics of evading detection and capture. They are also often formidable warriors in their own right and, should the enemy try to capture them by

force, it can expect to have to work very hard to secure its prize. Yet special forces soldiers and airmen are captured and do have to endure the discomforts, boredom and sometimes horrors of detention. Ironically, it is their elite status which puts them in acute danger of this fate because their ability means that they are chosen for missions often deep within enemy territory and far from the safety net of back-up forces. Furthermore, their missions can be of such secrecy that, in some cases, they will not be acknowledged officially, a situation that all too often puts the soldier outside the protection of the fair-treatment guidelines of the Geneva Convention.

Since the development of the special forces during World War II, and the expansion in airforce personnel following World War I, more and more elite units have been recognising the seriousness of the threat of capture for its soldiers. Thus it is that most elite units in modern military nations actively train their soldiers in the techniques of escape, evasion and detention survival. All fighter or bomber pilots are trained in how to survive for several weeks in hostile territory while waiting for a rescue attempt. Organisations such as the British Joint Services Intelligence Unit (JSIU) specialise in teaching British soldiers how to survive the psychological and physical challenges of torture and forced isolation. US Special Forces troops undergo the SERE course, which gives them the ability to survive should they be cut off deep behind enemy lines, or captured and placed in violent detention.

Such programmes of training are much needed. During the Vietnam War alone, some 586 US pilots were either captured or went missing over North Vietnam during attack raids there. More recent conflicts such as the Gulf War saw SAS personnel taken prisoner by the Iraqi forces and subsequently having to survive the most appalling attempts to extract information. Those that return from such imprisonment often recount the most dreadful depredations and conditions, and tortures which would break the most iron will. So it is that the modern training in the psychology of detention, escape and evasion produces some of the toughest courses in the world. Their aim is to make men and women who are capable of withstanding cruelty and psychological violence from their captors without giving up their vital knowledge and lethal skills. Cruelty and

suffering are actually built into the training to give the elite as real a taste as possible of the life of a captive without actually risking their lives (although, as we shall see, death in training is a precarious possibility). This chapter is about this training.

DETENTION

For a special forces soldier, capture by the enemy is sometimes held as the worst possible outcome of an engagement, with some holding it as even worse than death. If the enemy understands the nature of the operative it now holds – and usually they will because of the circumstances and place of the capture – their total priority will be to extract as much valuable information out of that person as possible. Many regimes around the world pay scant attention to human rights and so torture will often feature as a tool for extracting information should the soldier be unwilling to share his knowledge (and, with elite soldiers, that is almost always the case). Thus a terrible battle begins, the captor using all the means at his disposal to pull information forcibly from the captive's lips and the captive relying on his training, but more importantly his strength of will and intelligence, to resist divulging vital facts.

Whatever the mental strength of the captive, in the hands of an intelligent interrogator, the odds are stacked against him. Many countries invest as much time and science into investigating how to make people talk as others do in resisting interrogation. Furthermore, expert interrogators will usually know exactly what type of training the individual has had for this situation and so can modify their techniques accordingly.

Ultimately, being an elite captive is about participating in a cruel and lonely mental game in which personal resilience is the vital factor in holding out against interrogation. We shall look at how this resilience is fostered by elite units in a moment, but first we should examine the circumstances of deten-

Evasion mentality

Evasion is a claustrophobic, frightening experience, needing the patience to be concealed and make small movements towards one's goal of escape when safe to do so.

tion for elite soldiers in order to gain a true picture of what they face.

The Enemy Against
When we think of the horrors of detention, we tend to give priority to the experience of torture. Yet this is only one possible element of detention and far from the most common. From the point of view of psychological resistance, everything about military detention is usually geared to sap morale and motivation at every level, and leave the captive

bored, lonely, uncomfortable and confused. Once the captive is in this condition, it is easier for the captors to apply a bit of extra pressure to break the captive's will.

There are several general elements in particular which threaten the mental stability of a captive in a prison situation where rules of humanity do not apply. We shall examine the main ones here.

Loneliness and Boredom

Soldiers tend to be people who, up until the point of capture, have enjoyed full and dynamic lives in a social group of strong personalities and constant interest. Captors often realise this and so tend to place elite soldiers in places where they are isolated from human contact, the only people they see usually being their captors. The place of their confinement is frequently very small, offering little free movement and, without human contact, several unfortunate mental problems can start to develop. First, the soldier can start to withdraw into himself so that the outside world becomes less real. This allows the captors to begin drawing information from the prisoner because somehow the information handed over seems of diminished importance.

A further problem is that of prisoner dependency. Because the only human contact the prisoner receives is that of the guards, the ironic result is that the prisoner actually comes to look forward to the guards' visits, especially if the captors deliberately send friendly faces who talk with the

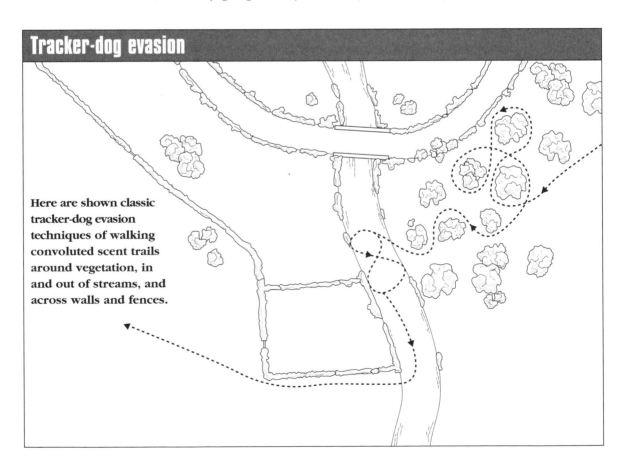

Tracker-dog evasion

Here are shown classic tracker-dog evasion techniques of walking convoluted scent trails around vegetation, in and out of streams, and across walls and fences.

Reading the liar

With an expert interrogator, the soldier must avoid the physical clues to lying. Touching the face or focusing eyes upwards can indicate the stress of lying.

Of course, detention is such that the soldier can even be in a communal cell and still feel lonely. During severe imprisonment, individuals tend to start looking after themselves more than others (although there are many examples to the contrary). Reports from inmates of the Nazi concentration camps often spoke of a ghost-like quality of detachment from one another, as fear and anxiety took hold and made people withdraw within themselves. Boredom is a problem which compounds this situation. Often the captive will not have access to anything remotely mentally stimulating and this in itself will cause time to draw by crushingly slowly. Boredom causes physical discomfort as the mind makes the body fidget in an attempt to relieve the monotony. This is turn leads to a build-up of anxiety which, given some months to run, can easily crush the will to carry on.

Fatigue

There are two essential causes of fatigue in a detention centre or prison camp. One is work. Prisoners of war are often put to work as a source of free labour, doing everything from constructing roads to making ammunition for the enemy war effort. A grim example from history is the Burma–Thailand railroad network which was constructed by Allied POWs and native labourers during World War II, in which the level of labour forced by the Japanese resulted in the deaths of some 102,000 prisoners. Although not all places of detention force such levels of labour, many do work the prisoners hard. The hard work is usually not supported by proper nutrition or adequate rest, so the prisoners start to suffer from intense fatigue that can soon tip into illness or mental despair. At the other extreme, enforced inactivity will have a similar result. The human mind tends to follow the actions of the body. Try sitting very still for a few hours with limited options for movement or entertainment. Your mind will

prisoner. This again may make the prisoner more willing to divulge information, if only to prolong the contact with the enemy visitor. The longer the prisoner spends in detention, the further removed he can feel from his family and friends, and the more despairing of his situation. Thus any degree of warm human contact is likely to become desirable and the enemy interrogators may cleverly fill this gap.

Effects of boredom

Boredom can be a great enemy in captivity. If the soldier can't find a way to cope, after only four days he will be fearful and apathetic in equal measures.

start to feel very tired in spite of no physical energy being expended.

Illness and Poor Nutrition

Military prison camps tend to produce weak, undernourished individuals who are prone to the inevitable illnesses that occur when many men are stuck in cramped, unsanitary conditions for long periods of time. A poor diet results in a suppressed immune system, so the prisoner is much more likely to contract illnesses – and they tend to be serious should he do so. The presence of serial illness is primarily a physical problem, but it has major psychological impact by lowering the prisoner's sense of self-esteem as his appearance and strength lose their vitality.

These factors are just a few of the general elements that assault the mind of an inmate under the detention of the enemy. Such conditions are faced by almost all those captured by an enemy and they can, for the unfortunate, be the thin end of the wedge which leads up to starvation, active cruelty and torture. Elite soldiers are more likely than, say, an army cook to attract the attention of the special interrogator. His (or her) purpose is to use physical or psychological methods to induce the captive to talk. As we shall see, the interrogator's 'skills' and tools can be very powerful indeed.

TORTURE AND INTERROGATION

One of the first methods of the interrogator relates to the room in which the prisoner is kept. US prisoners in Vietnam's infamous 'Hanoi Hilton' found themselves in squalid, tiny cells, often almost pitch black, with no toilet facilities and full of rats, cockroaches and huge spiders. The prisoner thus becomes soiled by his own waste and has to constantly fight off the often aggressive wildlife. Also, the rats and other creatures enjoy a freedom of movement which he cannot, placing his status, in effect, below that of vermin. Although the cell may seem a place utterly forgotten by human hands, it is important to the interrogator as somewhere which the prisoner will long to escape from, hopefully by divulging information. The prisoner will also be 'softened up' by having to listen to the cries of torture victims from other cells. Sometimes these are real, sometimes not, as many states have made use of recordings supposedly of the prisoner's fellow inmates being tortured during interrogation, though these are actually impersonations.

The interrogator, however, may choose a different environment for the prisoner, one which focuses more on sensory deprivation. This is usually a featureless cell without natural light (thus the prisoner loses track of time and date), without noise and where there is absolutely nothing to do. Clothing is also selected to be very soft so as to create little sensation on the skin. Research has shown that sensory deprivation is actually one of the cruellest tortures of all. Subjects undergoing sensory deprivation experiments started to show symptoms of behaviour abnormality after only 16 hours. After several days, the subjects were repeatedly hallucinating, disorientated, alternating between deep lethargy and hyperactivity, and suffering from extreme symptoms of fear and worthlessness. They particularly fell prey to any pre-detention mental fears.

Both the filthy cell and the sensory-deprivation environment help the interrogator to demonstrate his absolute power over the captive's life. He can then progress to ask-ing the prisoner direct questions backed up by various methods of coercion – torture, in short. Before we look at torture, it is worth reminding ourselves of the non-violent method of 'brainwashing'. This was often used to extract a renunciation of the soldier's war aims for propaganda and was effectively practised by the North Koreans and Chinese during the 1948–50 Korean War, and by the North Vietnamese during the Vietnam War.

During brainwashing, the captive will usually be placed in civilised but uncomfortable surroundings (such as sat on an armless, hard chair which is too small for him and facing a window with direct sunlight coming through). There he will meet a smart interrogator who will begin lengthy discussions about the conflict in which the soldier is involved. The interrogator will generally excuse the soldier's participation in the war and put the blame on the government of his home nation. The interrogator will then proceed to back up his case not by waving Marx under the prisoner's nose (this is far too unsubtle), but by showing anti-war literature produced in the prisoner's home country itself (Time magazine was often used during the Vietnam War). Other material such as information about tax rises in the prisoner's home state or country is also used to make the prisoner feel less affectionate about home government.

By these methods, and through keeping the conversations going for many hours, the interrogator can hopefully whittle away the prisoner's belief in his initial war aims and make a conversion. He is also trained to pick up on the physical traits someone displays when he or she is lying. These include evasive eyes (particularly if they look upwards, often indicating that the person is accessing their imagination, rather than their memory) and a nervous wiping of the mouth or nose while the lie is being told. However, if the mental interrogation is not successful (it is often not attempted for it is a time-consuming and skilled job), the interrogators will resort to more physical means such as those outlined below.

Torture

Torture comes in a whole spectrum of shapes and forms, too many to document here. However, there are several principles a 'skilled' torturer will apply. First, the level of torture is usually built up in gradual increments, thus keeping the prisoner in a state of constant terror about the next session. Secondly, the torture is backed by descriptions of what is happening to the prisoner's

Deprivation

Many prison cells are deliberately constructed to break the prisoner's will and make the interrogator's job easier. Sources of light are small and inadequate. The prisoner will often have no toilet facilities and so is forced to live in his own waste. Vermin and insects are often introduced to emphasise their freedom over the prisoner's confinement. Finally, the guards will degrade the cell even further in order to illustrate that they have complete control over the destiny of the prisoner.

body and what will happen in the future. Thus the torturer may say that he is going to cut off the prisoner's thumbs and proceeds to tell the prisoner what life will be like without opposable grip if he does not talk. Thirdly, the torture will mix the infliction of pain with the infliction of panic. A common example of the latter is to pull a towel over the victim's head and keep it soaked with water. Breathing under the towel slowly becomes impossible and the sensation of slow asphyxiation induces tremendous panic and fear which cannot be controlled. Using these three techniques, the torturer will keep his prisoner in terrible pain and fear, but keep emphasising how easy it would be for him to stop the treatment by simply opening his mouth. Any snippet of information given results in an instant diminution of the pain. Thus, like a dog being trained, the captive comes to associate talking with reward and, if the pain is severe enough, the temptation to divulge information is enormous.

Mental torture comes in as many different forms as physical torture and is just as destructive. Returning to communist brainwashing, one technique to emerge from the Korean conflict was the classic 'good cop/bad cop' routine', in which one quietly spoken and unthreatening interrogator would be replaced by a manic screamer who would bellow abuse in the prisoner's face. These two would then keep rotating their routines, disorientating the prisoner and naturally leading him to talk to the 'good cop' to keep him there longer, instead of the frightening opposite number. Humiliation is also an important factor in mental torture. Prisoners are usually kept stark naked and cold for each session, and female personnel are often invited in to make filthy disparaging remarks about the soldier's physique. This worthlessness gives the prisoner - if he does not mentally resist - an acute sense of his vulnerability and an awareness of the power of his captors.

Set against this are some even more extreme forms of mental torture. Blasting the prisoner with indecipherable noise at a deafening pitch for hour after hour before plunging him into total silence causes intense mental pain and confusion. The same effect is achieved by setting the prisoner within an environment of startling flashing lights. In both cases, intense head pain, nausea and disorientation result, and the prisoner will start to become desperate to get out of these unreal and hallucinatory environments.

Other Methods

An imprisoned elite forces soldier has to be on his constant guard for the stool pigeon – someone inserted into the cell or camp by the enemy to look like a neutral party (such as a fellow prisoner), but who reports back to the interrogators about his conversations. The 'double agent', as it were, will be made to look as realistic as possible to the situation and will often have a very detailed knowledge of the soldier's home culture and a perfect command of the language.

As an alternative to trying to break the soldier's will, some interrogators will attempt to bend the soldier's mind artificially with substances. Drug interrogation is something for which the elite soldier can do little to prepare. The list of drugs used is extensive and what they tend to do is not make the soldier tell the truth, but predispose him to talking more easily. This can be done through making him drowsy and less in command of his own voice, through making him hyperactive and garrulous, or through inducing feelings of anxiety or unreality which make him less committed to defending his information.

As we have seen, the array of methods and devices arraigned against the captured soldier is formidable in the hands of those prepared to use them. So what can the soldier do against such fearsome odds? How do you prepare the mind for detention and interrogation by the enemy?

DETENTION TRAINING

Training a special forces soldier for surviving detention and interrogation follows the primary rule for any type of military training: the training must be realistic enough to replicate the real experience, but without putting the soldier in any actual physical danger. One of the best examples of interrogation training is that conducted for the SAS by the Joint Services Interrogation Unit (JSIU). Based in Ashford, Kent, in the United Kingdom, the JSIU is manned by SAS soldiers and other personnel. It provides interrogation training for all the major UK forces, focusing mainly on elite units at risk from capture such as Royal Air Force pilots, special forces and units such as the Royal Marine Commandos and the Parachute Regiment.

During SAS training, the JSIU step in towards the end of the escape and evasion part of the training programme. Their mission is to put the SAS candidate through a punishing series of psychological and non-damaging physical tortures to see if the soldier has the mental resilience to withstand capture – if he has not, he will have failed to enter the SAS regiment. Much of the actual detail of what goes on during this part of training is protected by the Official Secrets Act, but insights have started to emerge from personnel who have been through the course. The staff of the JSIU make the scenario as realistic as possible, often dressing in the uniforms of possible captors and speaking in foreign languages. Treatments recounted by former candidates include:

- A towel is placed over the head and soaked with water (as described above), the towel only being removed when the 'prisoner' is on the verge of losing consciousness.

- A 24-hour period of interrogation is carried out in which the prisoner is subject to bright flashing lights and blaring white noise for long periods, resulting in a high degree of disorientation and fear.

- The JSIU staff conduct a beating in the next cell to the prisoner, with horrible sounds of impact, pain and vomiting. The object of the beating is actually a mattress and the JSIU personnel make the sounds of terror.

- The prisoner is stripped naked and verbally abused by a large panel of 'captors', including female personnel. Often the prisoner is left naked in cold conditions for hours before the interrogation, shrinking his penis, which then becomes the object of much derision.

- One scenario recounted involved a prisoner being shackled to a railway line in a siding. Then the interrogators pretend that they have made a mistake and there is actually a train coming (this is true, although the carriage is actually on another line). Despite seemingly frantic efforts on the part of the interrogators to unshackle the soldier, at the last second, they call off the attempts and pretend to run away. The prisoner's reactions are then judged as to the clarity of his thinking and reaction.

- The prisoner is tied to a board and dunked under water for periods of about 20 seconds before being brought up for air.

The brutal training of the JSIU has attracted some controversy (in one instance, an SAS soldier had his arm broken after being thrown from a moving lorry), but it doubtless has taught a generation of soldiers valuable lessons about themselves and about surviving detention. Similar courses are run throughout the world for special forces troops and, combined with the analysis from returning POWs, there is a growing general body of knowledge about the best way to stay sane and true in detention.

Much of this comes down to a simple issue of will and determination. To survive such terrible experiences as torture and isolation, the soldier must have a strong character to keep a sense of himself and also maintain hope for release. Character cannot be taught, but some principles can. Examples are:

● **Control what can be controlled.** Set up as much of a routine as possible, perhaps holding discussion groups with colleagues at certain times or simply

cleaning one corner of the cell. Use any unsupervised periods to remind yourself of who you are and what you are capable of, so take charge of any aspects of your life in detention that are not controlled by your captors.

● **Keep fit.** Keeping fit in detention is not always easy, especially if you are held in cramped conditions and the food is poor. Fitness helps the mind to stay stronger, so try to maintain some form of exercise programme. However, be cautious about burning up more calories than you can afford and rest if injured. If you are in very cramped conditions, simple stretching exercises and basic arm and leg strengthening exercises will

Non-violent interrogation

The prisoner sits, dirty and worn out, on a low stool, while the interrogator is smartly dressed on a tall seat. Lighting is arranged so that it is in the prisoner's face. Questioning is relentless and nimble, usually backed by the threat of return to torture.

Survival shelter

Constructing a survival shelter provides a break from the act of evasion. However, the soldier must not start to prefer its false sense of security over active escape.

stop muscles from wasting and help the mind stay healthier.

- **Keep the mind alert.** Mental alertness is extremely difficult to maintain when isolated and bored. Try to develop mental projects for yourself – such as writing a novel in your head (doing, say, a chapter each day) or planning a business idea – anything to keep the brain processes animated. Doing such mental tasks will also make you feel that your own personality and intelligence are not lost in the experience of captivity.

- **Do not encourage beatings.** Being aggressively defiant towards the captors is generally inadvisable as, if you attract further physical abuse, that will impair

your fitness and hence your survivability. Be as cunning as possible with your captors. Strike up conversations with ones who are in any way friendly – this personalises you in the captors' eyes and may make them less willing to harm you and it may even bring about better treatment.

- **Develop support networks.** If you are in the company of other prisoners, try to maintain the formalities of rank and military structure (although beware of giving away rank information to your captors). Rely on each other as support during times of interrogation and, if possible, design co-operative tasks between you to keep a sense of social interaction.

- **Plan to escape.** Even if escape might be verging on the impossible, it is still valuable to plan such an attempt. This is not only because it may well come to fruition, but also because it gives you a certain sense of strength over your captors and keeps the mind alert and lively as well.

By following these principles and mental activities, a period in detention can be made, if not exactly bearable, certainly slightly less harsh. A lot of these activities require good self-discipline to pursue and this is again where character comes in. The main point is not to become dependent upon the prison environment and to keep enough dignity to assure yourself that this is not where you belong.

ESCAPE AND SURVIVAL

There are no hard and fast rules about escaping from imprisonment. Indeed, it is not always productive in itself and may have severe repercussions for those left behind. Yet the prospect of escape can provide a psychological tingle that is a tremendous motivator to survive detention. A successful escape plan thrives on luck as much as judgement, but the thought processes should dwell on some of the following factors. Watch out for any patterns in the prison which you can use to your advantage, such as times when there are less guards on duty or when vehicles make deliveries. Remember these patterns and build up a profile in your mind of how the prison operates and when or where there are security lapses. This also involves utilising acute observation skills. Keep eyes and ears open at all times to gather more and more information to add to your stock of knowledge and try to get friendly guards inadvertently to reveal crucial information.

You must also have a plan. Escape can be about a moment of seized opportunity, but even if this does occur, you should have planned in detail what your course of action will be. Planning helps the mind to stay in focus and effectively acts as training for the escape event. Rehearse the escape in your mind time and time again, introducing various disasters to test out the efficiency of your plan. This basic mental preparation can help give drive and motivation during an escape attempt, but even if such an attempt should be initially successful, there is still the problem of how to survive during the flight to safety and how to evade capture.

EVASION AND SURVIVAL

Evasion is a skill taught to most troops as it applies not only to those who have escaped, but also to those who have yet to be caught. The practicalities of actually how to evade capture are covered in other books, but less is said about the mental requirements for evasion. Surviving in the wild while trying to evade capture is an extremely demanding mental situation. The body will quickly become tired and dirty, which itself can impair the thought processes and lead to depression and demotivation. Fear may also prey on the mind – the fear of what will happen to you if you are captured or recaptured. Importantly, your training should have made you aware of how the environment will attack the thought processes and what mental indicators of impending illness you should be looking for. The psychological essentials of evasion are:

- Have a clear idea of where you are going. Uncertainty can lead to despair, so the soldier must have some idea of what his objectives are. These should be broken down into hourly, daily and weekly objectives so that time is tightly controlled.
- During the initial escape or evasion period, the soldier should try to put as much distance from his starting point as

Effects of heat, wet, cold etc

When evading the enemy, soldiers must avoid unnecessary exposure to the elements and dehydration, all of which can increase his tiredness and his chances of making a mistake.

more fluidity in his planning. Also, every kilometre walked can increase motivation to continue. Studies have shown that the nearer to the objective, the greater the motivation, so achieving distance is a positive factor for mental endurance.

● Use your intelligence and training to avoid the pursuers. If moving through a civilian area, try to look as natural as possible; carrying a spade or similar civilian item can help you to blend in as to others this gives you a status that makes you less unfamiliar. Try to stay away from children and dogs, these often being the first to pick up on strangers. If in the countryside, create convoluted tracks through woodland and in and out of streams so that tracker dogs will become confused and turn back on themselves. In ways such as these, you are using the psychological processes of the pursuers, civilians and animals against them and thus giving openings to develop your escape.

● Do not be so committed to putting distance between you and the pursuers (unless it is absolutely necessary) that you overlook the necessity to eat and rest. Both sleep deprivation and malnutrition will cause apathy, clouded thought processes and insecurity, all of which can lead to making mistakes and errors in judgement. So sleep when necessary for short periods and do not

possible. If only 8km (5 miles) are travelled from the starting point, that will give a possible 200 square km (78 square mile) area for the searchers to deal with (assuming that they are aware of the starting point and that all directions of travel are equally valid). Psychologically, the greater the distance from the beginning, the greater sense of options the soldier will have and the exert yourself trying to remedy minor discomforts if the energy could be better used elsewhere. Steal food if possible to maintain your energy supplies, but be careful not to leave any tracks or be detected.

Torture

Torture makes the soldier physically weak; reality then seems unimportant and thus confession feels detached from consequences in the world outside of the prison.

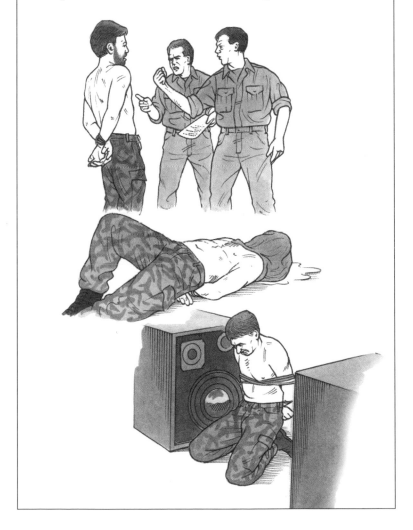

By looking after the body as much as possible, by having a plan and by fully entering into mind games with the pursuers, chances are the soldier will stay focused and committed to an escape attempt. Of course, this assumes that the soldier has a generally firm will. Regardless of training, the soldier attempting to escape must apply himself with a blind focus on the end result and learn to tolerate discomfort, pain and fear along the way. Thankfully for elite soldiers, their initial training period should have provided these skills anyway.

SURVIVAL

The final element of this chapter is that of survival. Being in a wilderness without food, shelter or water presents probably more of a danger to life and health than to those in pursuit. The actual techniques of survival are not really our focus here. Rather, what should be understood is how the environment affects mental processes and the will to survive.

The need for rest and food has already been discussed. Shelter is an equal priority. This applies even in warm countries because the two central enemies of anyone exposed are cold and heat. Exposure to extreme cold and extreme heat can lead, respectively, to hypothermia and hyperthermia. Hypothermia is a drop in body temperature

Skin heating techniques

The efficiency of this is best tested on your hands. If they are particularly cold, first touch them against a warm part of your body to gauge their temperature, then practise the following technique:

● First, imagine that the blood vessels in your hands have become wide open and that hot blood is pumping right through the hands and into the fingertips.
● While you are doing this, also imagine that you are immersing your hands in a thick, very warm orange liquid.
● Finally, while doing the above, actually look at your hands and believe that you have total control over all of your bodily processes.

If you follow the stages above, after one or two minutes the temperature of your hands should be warm, even hot if done successfully. Oriental practitioners of martial arts such as aikido and chi gong have long demonstrated the power of temperature change, a practice which is just starting to become accepted in the West.

---

below its safe core temperature range of 36–38°C (97.8–100.4°F), while hyperthermia is the opposite. Both can be fatal if not treated immediately and mental symptoms for both include deterioration in coherence, massive mood swings, withdrawal and inability to make decisions or absorb information. Yet even before this severe stage, cold and heat affect the mentally abilities of those in a survival situation.

The Effects of Cold

Studies were conducted as far back as World War I into the effects of cold on military skills. The loss of skin sensitivity and flexibility of the digits meant that marksmanship was severely disrupted. Further effects of cold later discovered were dips in attention, a reduction in the versatility of thought processes and the problems of having to balance the need to keep moving with the need to conserve energy. One fascinating product of studies conducted by the US Advanced Research Projects Agency in the 1970s was that psychologists found that skin temperature could actually be improved by up to 9°C (16°F) just by training soldiers to imagine heat

deflecting to the area in question. Personal testing of this training has showed me how achievable this is (see box for details of technique).

Extreme heat proves just as much of a challenge as extreme cold. The soldier will become tired and apathetic, and must follow common sense precautions such as staying out of the sun and drinking as much as possible. Psychologically, both heat and cold present the survival problem of generating fear, in that the soldier will start to think in terms of 'freezing to death' or 'dying of thirst'. This can actually speed the progress of these fates for, through mechanisms we still do not quite fully understand, the loss of willpower often results in a deterioration in health. Doctors have long noted that cancer patients become ill with greater rapidity once the diagnosis has been made and the term 'cancer' introduced.

Training can compensate for this effect by giving the soldier exact physical descriptions of the symptoms of cold and heat exposure and specific remedies. This enables the soldier to feel some degree of control over his illness. However, details of

Blending in

While in populated areas, the escaped soldier blends in by carrying an item, preferably trade-related, and avoiding children or animals (they can often spot strangers).

the advanced stages of the illness are often withheld from the soldier to avoid panicking should the symptoms be monitored.

The Desire to Live

In any survival situation, be it in a prison camp or on the run from pursuers, having clear goals and a strong desire to survive are possibly the most important tools the soldier has to come out of the situation alive. Training does impart essential skills of survival, but the lesson seems to be that character can be the determiner of whether someone lives or dies in a survival situation, and that may also be true of the fighting man as a whole.

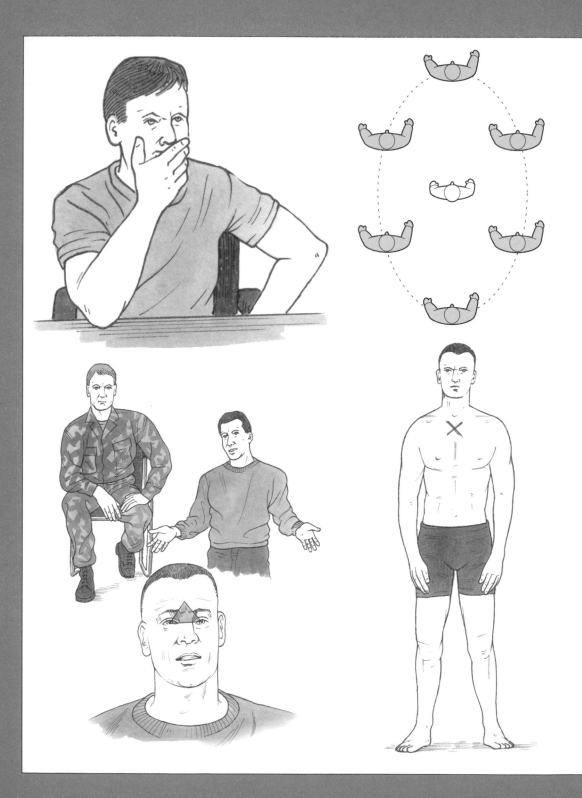

CHAPTER TEN

Peacekeeping and Diplomacy

Of all operational functions, peacekeeping and humanitarian work have become perhaps the likeliest destinations for the modern soldier. Although actual combat is unlikely, it is an ever-present threat, and soldiers have a vast array of other mental challenges to face in what is usually a confused and emotionally-charged environment and an alien culture.

The reasons for the growth in peacekeeping operations are politically and historically complex, and to a large extent revolve around the adoption of the role of the 'world's policeman' by the United States in particular and international organisations such as NATO and the United Nations. The fact now remains that few of the world's developed nations politically can afford to ignore world events in which images of suffering and helpless civilians are broadcast daily into the televisions of homes around the world.

For many soldiers, elite and regular, this has meant adjusting to a new environment of operations often situated somewhere between war and peace. Recent peacekeeping duties in places such as Sierra Leone, Bosnia, Kosovo and Somalia have placed soldiers in situations where they must perform a bewildering array of roles. These roles include separating warring factions, disarming those factions, providing food and medical relief, dispersing aggressive crowds and negotiating with local warlords. The list of duties is vast and so the mental qualities required of peacekeeping operations are similarly extensive. Combat skills alone are not enough, although they are essential. In addition, negotiating skills, knowledge of crowd psychology, ability to handle legal restraints, and the tact to care for trauma-tised civilians are just some of the extra skills a soldier must show in the peacekeeping and humanitarian role.

THE 'THREE-BLOCK' WAR

Peacekeeping has proved what the US Marine Corps calls the principle of the 'three-block war'. In the domain of low-intensity conflict, where violently opposed groups' factions can also see the peacekeep-ers as an unwelcome intrusion, soldiers can go from outright combat to humanitarian relief in the space of three blocks of a city centre. Thus peacekeeping soldiers must still possess the spirit of combat readiness at all times. A tragic illustration of this took place on 3 October 1993. The United States was at that time heavily involved in peacekeeping duties in war-ravaged Somalia. In an attempt to control the country's spiralling violence, a team of elite US Rangers and members of Delta Force were sent into the Somali capi-tal, Mogadishu, to apprehend Mohammed Farah Aidid, a local warlord. What was meant to be a 90-minute apprehension operation descended into a 17-hour bloodbath. Following the downing of a US Blackhawk helicopter, the US team found itself trapped in a nightmarish maze of intricate, claustrophobic streets while hundreds of armed Somali civilians and soldiers opened up on them with automatic weapons. In the utter chaos which fol-lowed, 18 Americans and more than 350 Somalis were killed, and 84 US servicemen were injured.

The incident in Somalia showed how the peacekeeping environment can escalate into violence within minutes. In this chapter, we will look at how elite and regular forces are now preparing their soldiers mentally for this alternative world of war.

THE DUTIES OF PEACEKEEPING

The list of duties that fall under the remit of peacekeeping operations is bewilderingly large. This is primarily because peacekeeping demands roles which are traditionally not those of the soldier. The US Army's Field Manual 100-23, *Peace Operations*, opens with a quotation from former UN Secretary-General Dag Hammerskold: 'Peacekeeping is not a job for soldiers, but only a soldier can do it.' Hammerskold's observation is insight-ful because, however orientated towards humanitarian relief, combat skills are still required to deal with the unpredictabilities of explosive civilian and military situations. What is needed by the military for these roles are men and women who are able to take the discipline of their combat training, but mix it with incredible flexibility both in thinking and the handling of people.

The manual goes on to list the multitude of occupations in which the soldier may find himself during a peacekeeping operation. The list includes some surprising tasks:

- diplomatic support
- preventing violence
- monitoring ceasefires and truces
- maintaining essential services such as water, electricity etc.
- investigating allegations of war crimes
- supervising the exchange of prisoners of war
- relocating refugees
- acting as mediators between belligerent parties
- building bridges and roads
- establishing protected zones
- apprehension of war crimes suspects

As we can see from this very partial list alone, the skills required by peacekeeping units are extremely broad. Furthermore, it is not just regular army units who are involved in these situations. Special forces are also widely utilised in peacekeeping operations. Elite troops bring with them specialist intelligence and combat skills which have a valuable place within missions aimed at restoring civil order. FM 100-23 states:

Special Forces (SF) assets deployed rapidly in denied or hostile areas can collect intelligence through area surveillance and reconnaissance. They can provide initial assessments in the areas of engineering, medical, security, and intelligence. With their language and area orientation, they can provide liaison with the local population, multinational forces, non-military agencies, and other military organizations. SF may assist in training and organizing local security forces. They may also enhance multinational interoperability by cross training with these forces. In humanitarian assistance operations, they can assist in providing and securing relief supplies. In peace operations, SF may execute precision strikes to destroy certain facilities and military capabilities by employing terminal guidance techniques for precision-guided munitions. SF may also be used to preclude or preempt terrorist activities and to conduct liaison with local militias.

As we can see, the talents of special forces in languages, counterinsurgency, surveillance and close protection all come to life within peacekeeping operations, as well as more conventional military roles.

The exhaustive scope of peacekeeping has drawn most elite units at one time or another into civil functions. Although some military observers have seen this as a dilution of traditional combat skills, most accept peacekeeping as adding a valuable new dimension into military thinking. The US Marine Corps has an alternative motto to their standard 'Semper fidelis' (Always faithful). This is 'Semper Gumby', Gumby being a flexible, bendy children's TV character popular with whole generations of US schoolchildren. The implication is obvious. The Marine Corps will bend and adapt to all manner of problems, military and civil, and peacekeeping is an ideal milieu in which to prove that capacity.

So what mental characteristics are required for a soldier to act as a successful peacekeeper? The US Army has defined a list of characteristics for the conduct of what it calls 'Operations Other Than War' (OOTW). These characteristics are:

- the objective
- unity of effort
- legitimacy
- perseverance
- restraint
- security

The Objective

Any soldier engaged in peacekeeping is generally faced with a situation that is confusing – mentally, morally and militarily. Thus it is imperative that the soldier forms a clear objective as to his actions and the actions of the group to give him direction and also stop the wasting of time and energy through diversions.

Unity of Effort

This is the team-mindedness spoken of in an earlier chapter. Peacekeeping requires a serious use of resources. In the Kosovo conflict, it was estimated that some three million Kosovan Albanians were displaced into neighbouring countries. To handle such an enormous influx of traumatised and destitute people, military units had to have clear and strong group interaction to make sure that relief efforts were coherent.

Legitimacy

Skills of tact, diplomacy and friendliness must be used to make the indigenous people accept the peacekeeping force as a legitimate one and accept its authority. This is easy to define, but difficult to achieve. Many Kosovan Albanians heralded the NATO troops who returned them to their villages initially as saviours, yet, once the troops prevented them from exacting revenge on Serbian homes, the Kosovans' attitude grew increasingly hostile. This is why combat skills are required – legitimacy sometimes has to be enforced.

Perseverance

Because peacekeeping operations have to deal with protracted problems, perseverance is an essential unit and individual attitude. Peacekeeping troops are still based in heavy numbers in the former Yugoslavia, many years after official hostilities ceased. The job of rebuilding trust between communities and preventing the flare-up of fighting requires a steady application of military presence and diplomatic pressure which cannot be rushed.

Restraint

Peacekeeping can be mentally cruel on the soldiers who participate in it. Many times their rules of engagement will specify that they cannot open fire during their missions, unless they are specifically targeted and fired upon, to avoid escalating the situation and adopting sides. In Yugoslavia, this meant that soldiers had to bury the innocent victims of massacres (including women and children) without being able to retaliate against the perpetrators of the war crimes. Such situations require personalities who can exercise considerable restraint and clearly follow the ROE (Rules of Engagement) laid down in their missions parameters.

Security

Security is defined by FM 100-15 as '[n]ever permit hostile factions to gain an unexpected advantage'. This is the active part of peacekeeping thinking – staying one step ahead of possible attacks and security infringements using conventional patrolling and combat techniques.

Added to these principles of OOTW are a host of other, more intimate psychological qualities which are needed for peacekeeping operations, all of which go to support the above. Chief amongst these as recommended by the US Army is the distinctive characteristic of being 'inquisitive'. Soldiers on peacekeeping operations are encouraged to find out as much as they can about the local culture with which they are dealing. This is not just to make them more broad-minded or better adjusted to handling the local population. It also serves to make soldiers more aware of any anomalies in their environment which might signify a possible terrorist threat (such as vehicular movement not consistent with the standard pattern of traffic, which could indicate a possible car-bomb attack).

Tact and Impartiality

Another pair of key qualities to advance is 'tact' and 'impartiality'. In the context of volatile civil relations, these attributes are essential. During the peacekeeping operations in Kosovo immediately after the repatriation of the Kosovan Albanian refugees, there were two major headaches for the peacekeepers. These were disarming the KLA fighters who had been fighting the Serbians and stopping the Albanian portion of the population exacting revenge on those Serbs who had stayed in Kosovo and not fled to Serbia itself. Justifying the protection of Serbs after the horrific war crimes perpetrated against many Kosovan Albanians was far

Reading aggression

The peacekeeping soldier should recognise signs of aggression. People stand up straight, place the hands on the hips and maintain a more direct eye contact.

Finger-poking, pushing and single-syllable threats are signs of impending violence. If these precede a sharp intake of breath, the soldier uses restraint techniques.

from easy and it required a firm, reasonable manner which demonstrated that the soldiers were not there to be partisan, but actually to maintain the peace.

Finally, the US Army (FM 100-23) advocates that soldiers practice 'imagination' and 'flexibility' during peacekeeping duties. Imagination, in particular, seems to be a curious recommendation, but both it and flexibility are concerned with a soldier's capacity for putting himself in another person's shoes and then deriving plans of action which are not set in stone, but which can adapt to the human elements of the problem.

As already stated, special forces soldiers are not withheld from becoming involved in peacekeeping missions. One of their main tactical remits is what are called Civil Affairs (CA) operations. CA units are not small – usually they operate at brigade strength to cope with the scale of humanitarian disasters – but they are expertly trained. A typical CA unit consists of language specialists, tactical squads and peacekeeping specialists, and their primary role is gathering information about the situation which is then relayed to the wider military and also to the various civil aid organisations present on the ground.

Unarmed combat point of focus

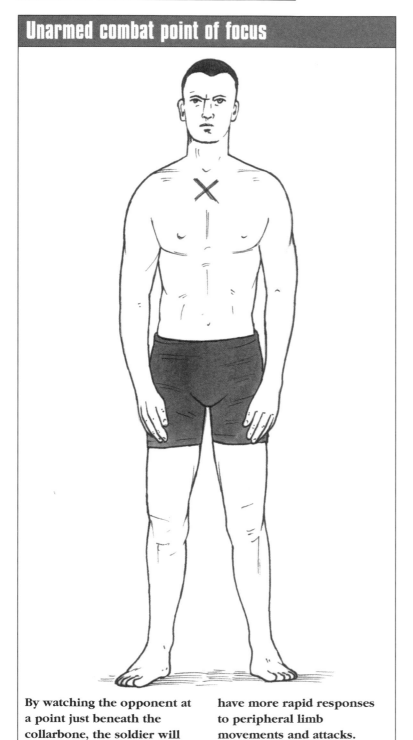

By watching the opponent at a point just beneath the collarbone, the soldier will have more rapid responses to peripheral limb movements and attacks.

Yet the case of the Rangers in Mogadishu shows that elite forces may also be called in in a more aggressive, combat-orientated role. The US Marines, for example (a good one, as they are heavily used in peacekeeping operations), are frequently applied as an advance body which enters a war zone or disaster area and uses bold military tactics to prepare the ground for the arrival of the conventional forces and civil organisations.

Each of the Marine Expeditionary Units (MEU) that enter a peacekeeping area will have already received realistic simulation training in coping with civil disorder and conflict. Members of the US Marine Corps are trained in 23 standard missions and one of these is an authentic training exercise in which actors play distressed crowds and the landscape is modelled accurately around a war-torn city. The training is so realistic that, in the words of Captain Lando Hutchens, on officer who has participated in several peacekeeping operations in Africa and Europe, the conditions they encounter for real 'don't surprise us'.

So far we have looked at the overall spectrum of mental qualities required for a peacekeeping soldier, but now we will turn our attention to two of the more demanding specific scenarios which a soldier may face on the ground during these delicate and exacting operations – crowd control and negotiation.

CROWD CONTROL

Crowds can be one of the most disorderly and unpredictable phenomena to face. This is not to say that a crowd of people may not be motivated by a clear and well-voiced idea. Yet, many soldiers will tell you that legitimate protest may all too easily turn into outright violence. Although rioting crowds may seem utterly without order, studies since World War II (especially those conducted in countries such as Northern Ireland, where civil disorder has been unfortunately commonplace) have shown that there are some patterns to how riots start, develop, are fought and are best controlled. The clash between soldiers and civilians is one which hangs on mental warfare, as more often than not the use of killing weapons is not an option or leads to political disaster.

Well before a crowd actually gathers, something has to bring them together. This is usually the role of the media, whether state-controlled or in the hands of the general populace. The ill-fated student pro-democracy protesters in Tiananmen Square in China did not have any access at all to the state television or radio, so they used hand-operated printing presses to publicise their intentions and also give instructions about the general direction of the movement. This is what is described as a 'planned' crowd, a group of people with a specific idea about what they are doing. The other reason for crowd gatherings is in the aftermath or expectation of a dramatic event (an accident or a football match being obvious examples). These are 'unplanned' gatherings and can be just as volatile as the more controlled version.

The problem in both cases is that, once a crowd is gathered, it starts to attain a life of its own. This is best put by the US Army's own document on crowd control, *Civil Disturbance* (FM 19-15):

Simply being a part of a crowd affects a person. Each person in a crowd is, to some degree, open to actions different from his usual behavior. Crowds provide a sense of anonymity because they are large and often temporary congregations. Crowd members often feel that their moral responsibility has shifted from themselves to the crowd as a whole. Large numbers of people discourage individual behavior; the urge to imitate is strong in humans. People look to others for cues and disregard their own background and training. Only well-disciplined persons or persons with strong convictions can resist conforming to a crowd's behavior. Crowd behavior influences the actions of both the disorderly participants and the authorities tasked to control them.

The task facing a group of peacekeeping soldiers when confronted by a large crowd gathering on a street is to stop the crowd behaviour gathering in aggression and emotion such that it suddenly starts to express itself in violence. The catalysts for this ugly turn are many:

● Specific individuals may encourage the crowd to turn to violence by using inflammatory speeches.
● The crowd may redirect what it feels is a legitimate anger against a third party towards those controlling the crowd, these then becoming the object of their hatred.
● The crowd may simply be taken to greater and greater heights of emotion

until it can no longer control itself and bursts into violence.

- Two or more crowds with opposing views may confront one another. Ironically, if the parties try to fight one another, both will turn their violence on those who try to stop the fighting (that is, the peacekeepers).

Once a riot gets out of control of the soldiers, the results can be frightening. On 30 January 1972 in Derry, Northern Ireland, some 20,000 civilians took part in a mass protest against the British policy of internment without trial. The march began in what was described by some afterwards as a 'carnival atmosphere', but when the march moved into William Street, stone-throwing began. The targets for the missiles were soldiers from the British Parachute Regiment. The soldiers were embarking on an arrest mission in the Bogside area of Derry when the incipient riot became more and more vitriolic. Thirty minutes later, and for reasons that are being legally debated to this day, the soldiers had shot dead 13 men and injured 13 others with their high-powered 7.62mm SLR rifles. What had begun as a legitimate protest, authorised by law, had ended in what would become forever known as 'Bloody Sunday'.

The experience in Derry all those years ago was precipitated by many different factors: the anger of the crowds; the context of violence that hung over Northern Ireland's daily life; fatigue and lack of proper riot-control training in the soldiers. Nor is it an isolated incident. During the Vietnam War, the United States saw student anti-war protestors being shot dead by soldiers from the National Guard at Kent State University. So, with the benefit of hindsight, how should a soldier think and behave during a crowd disturbance?

Studies conducted for the US Army have shown that soldiers who face riots are susceptible to several mental dangers. The first is that they will also get caught up in the excessive emotion of the crowd and start to be led by their feelings, rather than their judgement. This can lead to a soldier jettisoning his sense of restraint and acting impulsively, something very dangerous when he has weaponry. The key point is that riot-control soldiers and especially their leaders must have an iron grip on their emotions, remain self-aware and not allow themselves to be carried with a flow of emotions. One particular responsibility of the leader is to make sure that he moves amongst his men addressing them by their names repeatedly. This clarification of names stops the soldiers losing their own personalities in that of the crowd and therefore keeps them thinking about their commitments.

Verbal Abuse

The soldiers who confront a riot also need to be mentally prepared for some of the psychologically disturbing tactics that the crowd may use against them. Verbal abuse is likely to be very personal and ferocious, and will often focus on criticising the soldier's moral position in relation to the rioters. The soldier must adopt a distance from any comments made and only judge the rioter's abuse in the context of tactical developments (there will be plenty of time for reflection once the riot has been controlled). This can be extraordinarily difficult. One soldier from Northern Ireland recounts how, after two of his friends had just been shot down in the street, he had to endure the chants of children only yards away giving the football score chant 'Two – nil'. Resisting a violent response to such provocation is incredibly hard, but vital.

As a further challenge to the soldiers, women and children may be placed in the front ranks of the crowd to intimidate them into non-resistance. Again, self-control must be used to avoid sympathising with a

Gestures to recognise in negotiation

When people feel defensive towards what you are saying, they will often make physical barriers across their body and face with their arms and legs. Here are three classic defensive gestures.

Negotiating gestures

**Leaning forward invites clo-
sure of a meeting, exposing
the palms implies honesty,**

**and focusing on the triangle
between eyes and forehead
implies concentration.**

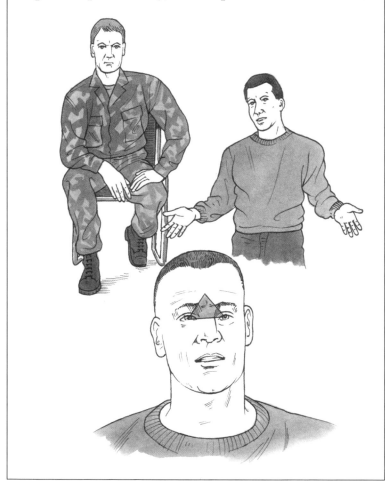

- Fireworks are dipped in glue and covered with nails or BB shotgun pellets to act as grenades.
- Nail-firing guns used in the construction industry are fired through thin pieces of plywood – the nail guns are designed to fire nails into solid con-crete, so the nail simply cuts straight through the plywood and flies onwards towards the soldiers.

More serious is when the riots are conducted in tan-dem with terrorist attacks. A classic tactic used by Republican terrorists in Northern Ireland was to position themselves ready with their weapons in a van behind the crowd. When the time was right, they would blow a whistle and the crowd would part before them. At this point, they would open fire on the British troops for a few sec-onds, before blowing the whistle once more, and allowing the crowd to close in front of them as a protective shield.

Naturally, the best way to defend against this type of attack, and against the dan-gers of the riot in general, is to get the riot-ers to disperse. Here some strong psycho-logical tactics are needed to break the crowd's emotional momentum. Any officer in charge of riot-control troops has a sliding scale of options for dispersing the crowd, ranging from withdrawal at one end of the scale to the use of deadly force at the other.

particular face, gender or age. Finally, the sol-diers should be prepared for all manner of weapons. Petrol bombs, stones and sticks are the most expected, but other inventive weapons have been created in riots:

- Balloons are filled with paint to use against vehicle windscreens.

However, the key principle is that the minimum force should be used to diffuse the situation. Indeed, studies have shown that the use of killing weapons generally leads to the precipitation of violence.

Colonel Rex Applegate, one of the United States' most robust military thinkers and an expert in both riot control and unarmed combat, came up with several psychological principles of crowd handling which are used to this day. Applegate's principles boiled down to several key tactics:

Riot control shotgun

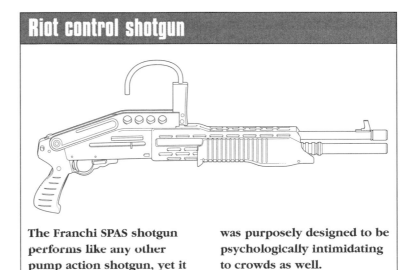

The Franchi SPAS shotgun performs like any other pump action shotgun, yet it was purposely designed to be psychologically intimidating to crowds as well.

- Display force at the earliest possible juncture. Note that the force is not actually used, but many crowds in the early stages of development will actually disperse if they suddenly find themselves confronted by large groups of well-organised and powerfully armed soldiers. Certain weapons can encourage dispersion. The SPAS shotgun (see illustration), for instance, is no more powerful than any normal shotgun technology, but its intended 'Mad Max' appearance can have a great deterrent effect upon would-be rioters.
- Use crowd control formations. Many different configurations are possible, but generally a solid wall of men, charging with riot-shields presented, can disrupt the confidence of even the most courageous crowd. The important principle appears to be that the soldiers should act as one, thus giving the crowd the impression that they are dealing with one solid force, rather than a collection of individuals.

- Rotate the soldiers regularly. If engaged for long periods of time in riot control, the soldiers will become mentally and physically exhausted. Once this occurs, the emotions are more able to take control during riot conditions. Taking soldiers regularly out of the 'front line' enables them to regain perspective and energy.
- Target the weakest members of the crowd. These tend to be located at the back, so applications of tear gas or other weaponry aimed at this point can cause the crowd to disintegrate from the 'tail to the teeth'.
- Give strong commands. Leaders must stand before the crowd with absolute confidence and give clear orders for dispersal. Many people instinctively succumb to authority figures and someone standing in front of them and refusing to back down may sap their momentum.

Applegate's views are much respected and are still taught today in military training. However, the modern soldier now also has an incredible array of non-lethal weapons at his disposal which also assault the mental force of a crowd. Some of these weapons have been around for decades. The water cannon, for example, remains effective not for blasting rioters out of the picture, but for the fact that people become less ardent and motivated once they are soaked and cold (self-interest kicks in again and this causes the crowd mentality to break up). Yet other weapons seem to come from the ranks of science fiction. A sound system is currently being developed which can send out deep vibrating musical notes beneath the audible range of the human ear. The powerful vibrations pulse through the rioter's bowels and cause involuntary defecation – few people would maintain rioting after this had occurred.

Deafening blasts of sound are also used to break up the rhythmic chants crowds often use to mobilise themselves and this sound has a double effect in that it often induces nausea, vomiting and severe head pains.

Whatever the weapons options available, nothing will replace a confident and resolute soldier as a riot deterrent. In this crucial peacekeeping role, personal courage and the resilience to stop oneself being immersed in group hysteria are enough to survive riot conditions, if not control them.

NEGOTIATION

From the very physical duty of riot control, we turn now to the equally vital peacekeeping responsibility of negotiation. This skill usually falls to officers when it comes to, say, acting as a mediator between two warring factions, but each soldier will usually encounter a situation where verbal intelligence alone will be vital in defusing a potentially violent situation. Most soldiers will be taught some level of negotiating

VIP protection 1 – analysing threats

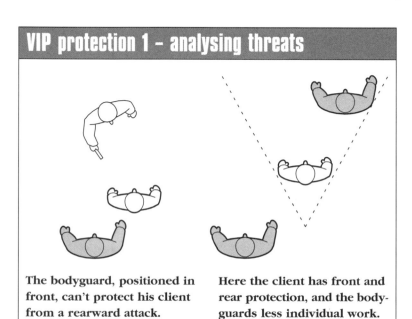

The bodyguard, positioned in front, can't protect his client from a rearward attack.

Here the client has front and rear protection, and the bodyguards less individual work.

The bodyguard shields the client from the rear and can respond to frontal attacks.

The V-shaped formation is used when trouble or attempts on the client's life are likely.

VIP protection 2 – giving protection

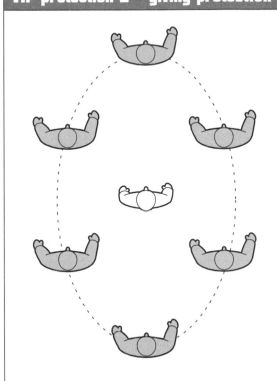

A double V for the very important. As a part of soldier's peacekeeping tasks, protection duties need an understanding of assassination countermeasures and crowd psychology.

skills when destined for a peacekeeping zone – elite soldiers may well be trained in these techniques to an advanced degree, as we saw in the case of counterinsurgency operations in the last chapter. Negotiating tactics are a very broad subject, but we can deal with some of the essentials here.

The key point that most soldiers are taught is that the first rule of negotiation is to genuinely listen to the grievances of all parties before starting to formulate proposals. This is where the maxim of 'impartiality' comes in. FM 100-23 defines why impartiality should be adhered to:

A force must guard against unequal treatment and avoid controversial, off-the-record remarks that may reach unintended audiences. These comments may lead to a demand for the offender's removal and, if reflecting a prejudice believed to be widely held in a national contingent, to pressure for the withdrawal of the entire national contingent.

Rushing to judgement tends to leave one party feeling that their reasoning has not been heard and consequently they are less likely to stick with the fine points of any agreement. True listening – or 'staring with ears', as it has been called – will also tend to bring down the aggression of an argument because the speaker will feel obliged to make his argument as coherent as possible.

Once the soldier has heard all sides of the argument, he must make up his mind as to whether it is within his jurisdiction to make a decision; if it is, he must stick to the principle of impartiality. Take the following imagined scenario:

A refugee family (husband, wife, two children under the age of four) has been resettled in their old village after a period of some six months of being dispersed during a civil war. Their neighbour (a 62-year-old man, widowed), though he did not actively participate in any action against the family, belongs to the ethnic group that committed most of the atrocities and ethnic cleansing against the family's people. The husband of the family claims that the man should therefore give up his land to them as a penalty for what his people did. If this is not done, then the husband (backed by a group of sympathetic relatives and friends) threatens to burn the neighbour's house to the ground. The old man, for his part, says he wishes

*nobody any ill, that he never partici-
pated in the war and that, as he has
lived in the house all his natural life, he
could never leave.*

This scenario is based upon actual cases encountered in Kosovo after the war there. Presented to the negotiator, this situation calls for the qualities of flexibility and imagination asserted by the US Army Field Manual. What is important is that the negotiator reflects on all the implications of any possible course of action. If he relocates the old man, will he be safe in his new destination and, being widowed, will he be able to look after himself outside of familiar surroundings? Can the army or relief agencies offer any financial assistance to the family in return for their tolerance of their neighbour? How soon will violence occur if no action is taken? If the family's request is granted, will it lead to other similar requests in the village? Only the soldier's intimate understanding of the local culture and the people involved will lead him to a decision. Yet, during the process of negotiation itself, there are several techniques he can apply that will make the negotiations more amicable.

Principle amongst these is a basic understanding of how body language works. Studying body language is no longer the preserve of the business world. A recent television recruitment advertisement for the British Army featured a squad of British soldiers confronting a group of armed African civilians around a well and asking for a drink of water. For some reason, we cannot tell because of the language barrier, the African men become agitated and start getting to their feet and menacingly toy with their weapons. The officer of the British troops then takes off his sunglasses, allowing the leader of the other group to see his eyes. The situation calms itself and the British soldiers are allowed to drink.

The advertisement was meant to show that to be an officer requires a good understanding of negotiating skills and body language techniques – people tend not to trust someone whose eyes they cannot see. As psychological understanding expands, more soldiers are receiving training in aspects of reading others' thoughts through the mannerisms of the human body and we can see how this might be valuable in negotiations.

For example, there is a sequence of body language gestures which is useful to watch out for in the other person. Although a person's words might be coming out steady and strong, their body may well give away the fact that they are lying. Typical signs are:

- Rubbing the mouth or nose when talking – If this is done only lightly, this is most likely a nervous action, rather than an itch. The person is in effect using the gesture to distract them and you away from the lie.
- Casting the eyes upwards when talking – People often look upwards when they are accessing their imagination, hence, if the person is not actually looking at something, he could be inventing what he is saying.
- Inability to maintain eye contact – This literally stems from the fact that the person subconsciously fears you will pick up on the lie as it is being told or that the person is too embarrassed to make eye contact.

Many of these signals we pick up automatically, but, in the situation of peacekeeping negotiations, the soldier must look out for them consciously to make sure that he is getting the truth from his interlocutor. By contrast, the soldier should adopt body postures which convey trust and reliability at every stage. When making a frank point, turning the palms upwards is a gesture of sincerity which travels well in most cultures.

Riot control

A psychological method of riot control used in places such as Northern Ireland involved placing a line in the path of the rioters, and announcing that anyone crossing the line would be shot.

Eye contact should be maintained, but not be intimidating – studies have shown that, for serious discussions, people make a triangular point of focus which has its base with the two eyes and its apex in the centre of the forehead. Generally, the overall body language in negotiations should be open and broad to convey trust and enthusiasm. If the soldier notices the person across from him has his arms and legs crossed, and that he is avoiding eye contact, this most likely means that the person is not happy with the way the conversation is proceeding. (People tend to cross parts of their bodies in front of themselves to form protective barriers when they are feeling threatened or tense, although they also do this when they are cold!) Through building up a profile of body language, the soldier in negotiations is able to at least read some of the emotional content behind what a person is saying, which is actually a better indicator of what they will do.

Whether in negotiation or standing behind a shield facing a riot, the peacekeeping soldier faces an environment neither civilian nor military, but which demands the best skills of both worlds. Peacekeeping and diplomacy are not traditional military tasks, but they are increasingly becoming the dominant form of operation for many of the world's soldiers, particularly those members of NATO and the United Nations. The volatility of world politics and the hints of wars to come suggest that armies will continue to need men who are capable of adapting their minds to the 'three-block war' and the need to use wits as much as weaponry.

CHAPTER ELEVEN

Future Wars

As we left the twentieth century, our understanding of military psychology seemed almost complete. Research conducted since 1945 means we now know most things about human behaviour in combat – from the effects of sleep deprivation to the psychological effect of artillery fire and ways of creating discipline. The question now is whether there is anything left to be discovered.

As we inch into the 21st century and look to the future of combat psychology, there is one area of development that will perhaps challenge notions of the warrior personality to a greater extent than any other has done so far. It is, in a sense, not a new area at all, but it is reaching such futuristic achievements that the 21st century will probably see the most significant overhaul of fighting technique and military mental skills since World War I.

This area is that of technology. It is doubtless that the 20th century changed the face of war through technological advance. In one century, this advance proceeded at a pace faster than in the previous four or five centuries put together. With each new weapon introduced, with each new piece of communications equipment utilised, the sol-

dier's role on the battlefield expanded and became more complex, and the speed of reactions required became faster. Whereas in World War I an artillery officer' firing patterns were based on observation and calculation, today's soldier can use satellite reconnaissance to pinpoint targets to within a few metres and destroy them with advanced ordnance at a range of 40–50km (25–30 miles). A good expression of the new demands of technology came from a US fighter pilot who had served in both World War II and Vietnam. 'In World War II, if you saw the enemy at a distance you had about ten minutes to start planning your evasive manoeuvres. In Vietnam, in the jets that we were using, you had about five seconds.' This fighter pilot was expressing what most modern soldiers now know: each advance in technology pushes up the demand for skills and reactions. It is into this arena that governments have poured huge sums of money in order to discover ways in which they can maximise the effective human use of such complex combat technology.

LONG RANGE COMBAT

One result of advancing military technology for the common soldier is that, in many ways, he is becoming more distant from the enemy he confronts. Artillery, missile and air ordnance delivery have become so sophisticated that the only contact some soldiers will have with their enemy will be a blip on a computer screen prior to pressing the launch button. Attack-helicopter pilots who served in the Gulf War often remarked on how much the convoys they were destroying looked like figures in a computer game as they peered at them through their thermal imaging cameras and head-up display units (the latter projects combat and cockpit information onto the inside of the pilot's visor). And yet, there were still soldiers on the ground and tanks in action, engaging the enemy, taking prisoners, burying the dead. Some conflicts, such as that in Kosovo, have shown up the limits of current technology in taking on an enemy consisting of individual men attacking small villages with assault rifles and machine guns. As such, the lesson of the 20th century seems to be one of caution about presuming that traditional combat skills are no longer needed. There will always be situations in which there is no substitute for a highly trained individual on the ground to make decisions at a human level.

However, technology has a habit of surprising us. New types of weaponry and communications are appearing all the time and many scientists are chasing

Humanitarian work

Soldiers are increasingly called upon to act in humanitarian roles, needing mental and social skills perhaps not required of many earlier generations of soldiers.

after new methods of conducting war that theoretically could dispense with a human battlefield presence altogether. An example of this is the Boeing X-45A. This is an experimental ground-attack aircraft which is intended to deliver anti-radar missiles and high-explosive ordnance with exceptional manoeuvrability and high speed, and all without a pilot. That is not strictly true: the 'pilot' will be sat in front of a computer screen potentially thousands of miles away, controlling the aircraft remotely.

Unmanned aircraft are nothing new. Unmanned reconnaissance planes were developed after the U-2 spy jet piloted by Gary Powers was shot down over the Soviet Union in 1960. Since then, they have performed usefully in conflicts such as the Gulf War and Kosovo. The difference with the X-45A is that, in carrying weapons, it heralds the automation of a job previously regarded as the sole preserve of human beings. This will be controversial, but the arguments for the X-45A and its type (Unmanned Combat Aerial Vehicle – UCAV) are robust. UCAVs are predicted to be 75 per cent cheaper to operate and they can manoeuvre in patterns that would kill a human pilot with G-force. Also, training the terminal operator would be considerably cheaper than the $2 million currently spent on training pilots in the United States ($1 billion a year is spent in the United States purely on maintaining the skills of F16 pilots).

The fact is, however, that, if the X-45A reaches production stage and exceeds human pilot ability, military recruiters and psychologists will have to start looking for a new type of 'virtual warrior'. The operator of the X-45A would be using two flat-screen monitors, one showing cockpit information, and the other a digital 3D image of the battlespace. Thus, what the military would require is not a person who can endure great physical stress and still

The technological soldier

Uniforms are no longer items of clothing, but have become kit which enhances the soldier's mental and physical performance, including eyesight, temperature-control and hearing.

function, but someone who can operate a computer terminal under great mental pressure, without actual threat to his life, and still remain focused, attentive and aggressive in action.

VIRTUAL WAR

This is what some commentators have called 'virtual war' and it is also spreading to land combat. Military technicians are already seeing unmanned tanks and mobile artillery pieces as distinct possibilities. Yet, even for those soldiering roles that require a man to physically be present on the battlefield, times are changing. In the United States at present, the army is experimenting with head-up visual display units which, like more advanced thermal-imaging goggles, allow a soldier to operate in zero-visibility conditions while receiving combat information projected onto the screen before his eyes. The soldier thus equipped would have knowledge beyond that of his senses – he could 'see' behind buildings and receive satellite data on the units facing him. Furthermore, advances are being made in thought-weaponry. Brain-scanning techniques have been developed over the past 20 years which enable a person to control simple mechanical processes just by thinking the action. The process is extremely complex and at present its potential is rudimentary. Yet, in the future, we can imagine a soldier who goes into combat without a trigger and with just his mind to control and fire weapons with lightning-fast response times.

Perhaps the extreme of the 'virtual war' scenario is those soldiers who will be trained purely to 'fight' in the cyberspace of computer terrorism. Almost every level of advanced world society runs upon computerised systems and one talented hacker could effectively destroy the infrastructure of a nation, if competent enough. In light of this bloodless threat, more and more military personnel are being shocked into action and have started training personnel to deal with this new threat. The shock to the system is great. Men who have traditionally considered an enemy to be fixed within a time, place and boundary are now facing an utterly nameless and faceless threat. This threat could be one individual with enough computer power to bring down an entire system of military logistics (recent international computer virus infections have shown us that this is perfectly possible).

FUTURE ROLE?

So where does the virtual war leave the elite soldier? Most authorities admit that there will always be a place for highly trained, highly motivated soldiers to do

Remote warfare

An unmanned reconnaissance vehicle in development by the US. More and more battlefield duties will be executed by machines over the coming decades.

The future warrior?

Today's soldier must adjust to the very different psychological pressures of delivering devastation from a computer screen. However, recent conflicts have shown that there is always the need for a real human presence at the actual place of battle.

some of a nation's less palatable jobs. Despite technological advances, there is no computer in existence to touch the human mind's ability to decipher chaos and deal with it in innovative ways. Yet what will occur is that a new breed of warrior, one who perhaps never even holds a gun, will have to be trained in the skills of computerised warfare such as never before. Such an individual will create new mental issues for world military forces. When sitting thousands of miles behind the front line, is an individual capable of maintaining the aggression which is needed for combat ? What are the psychological implications when war cannot be distinguished from a game in a computer? Does such a soldier need to be trained in traditional forms of combat at all?

The questions go on. However, what is certain is that the role of the soldier is changing and his mental skills must change adapt with it. In today's high-technology, ultra-fast war zones, individuals are required who can shift from a muddy battlezone to computer-terminal warfare in minutes and still retain their sense of the overall battle raging around them. This scene-shifting will require a mind of extraordinary flexibility and intelligence. We wait to see how the next generation of soldiers will look and behave.

index